THE TRUSTEE ACT 2000 –
A PRACTICAL GUIDE

D1352442

THE TRUSTEE ACT 2000 –
A PRACTICAL GUIDE

P J Reed
of Inner Temple, Barrister

and

R C Wilson
of Middle Temple, Barrister

JORDANS
2001

Published by
Jordan Publishing Limited
21 St Thomas Street
Bristol BS1 6JS

British Library Cataloguing-in-Publication Data
A catalogue record for this book is available from the British Library.

ISBN 0 85308 664 8

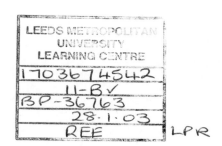
Typeset by Mendip Communications Ltd, Frome, Somerset
Printed in Great Britain by MPG Books Ltd, Bodmin, Cornwall

PREFACE

'To reach a conclusion on this matter involved the court in wading through a monstrous legislative morass, staggering from stone to stone and ignoring the marsh gas exhaling from the forest of schedules lining the way on each side. I regarded it at one time, I must confess, as a slough of despond through which the court would never drag its feet, but I have.'

Whilst the Trustee Act 2000 is not in all respects happily drafted, it is unlikely to inspire the sort of comment above which emanated from Harman LJ in respect of the Town and Country Planning Act 1959. Not all new legislation requires detailed commentary. The Sea Fishing Grants (Charges) Act 2000 springs immediately to mind. However, the Trustee Act 2000 seemed to us to merit a book, constituting as it does the most extensive overhaul of trust law since 1925. Thus it was that two chancery practitioners gave up their weekends, evenings and social lives for the year 2000.

The changes effected by the Act gave rise to a plethora of important issues, many practical and some academic. In writing what is intended to be a practitioner's guide, we hope that we have dealt with most of the former and at least some of the latter.

There is a great number of people whom we must thank. First of all, our families who have had to endure endless discussion of the changes to the Settled Land Act 1925. We would also like to thank our colleagues in chambers for the keen interest they have shown in the project, in particular Cenydd Howells and Christopher Cant whose impressive insight into the subject has been invaluable. Our thanks must also go to our clerks and our publishers for their help and support. We owe a particular debt of gratitude to Martyn Frost of Barclays Bank Trust Company for his enthusiasm, encouragement and remarkable ability to track down otherwise elusive source materials. In spite of all the help we have received, any errors or omissions are of course ours alone.

PENELOPE REED and RICHARD WILSON,
9 Stone Buildings,
Lincoln's Inn,
January 2001

CONTENTS

PREFACE   v
TABLE OF CASES   xi
TABLE OF STATUTES   xv
TABLE OF STATUTORY INSTRUMENTS   xxi
TABLE OF INTERNATIONAL LEGISLATION   xxiii
TABLE OF ABBREVIATIONS   xxv

Chapter 1   INTRODUCTION AND BACKGROUND   1
             Introduction   1
             The background to the legislation   1
             The Law Commission's principal recommendations   2
             Parliament   3
             Application and outline of the Act   4
             Commencement of the Act   8
             Some consequential and minor amendments 9
             Authors' view of the Act   10

Chapter 2   THE STATUTORY DUTY OF CARE   11
             Introduction   11
             The basic duty   11
             Application of the statutory duty of care   14
             Exclusion of liability   23
             Comparison with the 'common law' duty of care   26
             Comparison with the Trustee Act 1925, sections
             23(1), (3) and 30   28
             Claims for breach of the statutory duty of care   30
             Reviewing existing trusts   33
             Summary   35

Chapter 3   POWERS OF INVESTMENT   37
             Introduction   37
             Summary of the law under the 1961 Act   38
             The general power of investment   39
             The meaning of 'investment'   40
             Loans secured on land   41
             The Standard Investment Criteria   42
             Advice   45
             Checklist on the exercise of the general power of
             investment by a trustee   48
             Effect of authorised investment   49
             Statutory duty of care in relation to investments   51

	Scope of the general power of investment and contrary intention	54
	Application to bare trustees and implied trustees	56
	Summary	57
Chapter 4	**ACQUISITION OF LAND**	59
	Introduction	59
	The background to the reforms	59
	The new powers to acquire land	62
	Powers of the trustees once land has been acquired	64
	Duty of care	65
	Scope of the power	65
	Strict settlements	66
	Summary	69
Chapter 5	**AGENTS, CUSTODIANS AND NOMINEES**	71
	Introduction	71
	Summary of the old law	71
	The new regime	72
	Agents	73
	Nominees and custodians	81
	The duty to review	83
	Trustees' liability for the defaults of agents, custodians and nominees	84
	Other matters	85
	Delegation checklist	86
	Summary	87
Chapter 6	**REMUNERATION OF TRUSTEES**	89
	Introduction	89
	The law before the Trustee Act 2000	89
	Some specific problems	91
	Structure of the Act in relation to remuneration	92
	Where there is an express charging clause	92
	Where there is no provision in the trust instrument or legislation for charging	94
	Reasonable remuneration	96
	Professional capacity	96
	Administration of estates	97
	Remuneration of trustees of charitable trusts	97
	Trustees' expenses	98
	Remuneration and expenses of agents, nominees and custodians	99
	Summary	100

Chapter 7   INSURANCE   103
             Introduction   103
             The power to insure: the previous law   103
             The power to insure   104
             The duty to insure   106
             Summary   107

Appendix I   TRUSTEE ACT 2000   109

Appendix II PARLIAMENTARY STAGES OF THE TRUSTEE
             ACT   145

Appendix III PRECEDENTS   147
             Form A: Inclusion of statutory power in investment 147
             Form B: Investment on ethical grounds   147
             Form C: Clause excluding statutory power of
             investment   147
             Form D: Clause excluding power to acquire land   148
             Form E: Standard professional charging clause   148
             Form F: Agreement of trustees in writing that
             professional trustee should receive remuneration 148
             Form G: Particulars of claim (High Court) alleging
             breach of the statutory duty of care in respect of
             investment   149
             Form H: Particulars of claim (County Court)
             alleging breach of the statutory duty of care in
             respect of investment   151
             Form I: Defence to Form G (High Court) relying
             upon exemption clause   153
             Form J: Clause excluding the statutory duty of care 154
             Form K: Clause limiting the standard of care   154
             Form L: Investment policy checklist   155

INDEX   157

TABLE OF CASES

References are to paragraph numbers.

Armitage v Nurse [1998] Ch 241; [1997] 3 WLR 1046;
   [1997] 2 All ER 705, CA   2.42, 2.44, 2.45, 5.27

Bailey v Gould (1840) 4 Y&C Ex 221   7.11
Barber, Re (1886) 31 Ch D 665   6.9
Bartlett v Barclays Bank Trust Co Ltd (No 2) [1980] Ch 515; [1980] 2 WLR
   430; [1980] 2 All ER 92, ChD   2.8, 2.51, 3.51, 7.12
Betty, Re; *sub nom* Betty v Attorney General [1899] 1 Ch 821   7.5, 7.11
Binions v Evans [1972] Ch 359; [1972] 2 WLR 729; [1972] 2 All ER 70, CA   3.31
Boardman v Phipps; *sub nom* Phipps v Boardman [1967] 2 AC 46; [1966] 3
   WLR 1009; [1966] 3 All ER 721, HL   5.32, 6.5, 6.6
Bristol and West Building Society v Mothew (ta Stapley & Co); *sub nom* Mothew
   v Bristol and West Building Society [1998] Ch 1; [1997] 2 WLR 436; [1996]
   4 All ER 698, CA   3.47, 5.29
Burke, Re; *sub nom* Burke v Burke [1908] 2 Ch 248, ChD   3.61
Bunting, Re [1947] 2 NZLR 219   6.9

Carr-Glynn v Frearsons [1999] Ch 326; [1999] 2 WLR 1046; [1998] 4 All ER
   225, CA   5.29
Chalinder & Herington Solicitors, Re [1907] 1 Ch 58, ChD   6.8
Chambers v Goldwin (1804) 9 Ves 254   6.6
Cowan v Scargill [1985] Ch 270; [1984] 3 WLR 501;
   [1984] 2 All ER 750, ChD   2.2, 2.49, 3.29, 3.35, 3.54, 3.60
Cradock v Piper (1850) 1 Mac & G 664   6.6

Duke of Norfolk's Settlement Trusts, Re, *sub nom* Earl of Perth v Fitzalan-
   Howard [1982] Ch 61; [1981] 3 WLR 455; [1981] 3 All ER 220, CA   6.6

Earl of Perth v Fitzalan-Howard; *see* Duke of Norfolk's Settlement Trusts, Re
Edge v Pensions Ombudsman [2000] 3 WLR 79; [1999] 4 All ER 546; (1999)
   The Times, October 19, CA   3.54

Fry v Fry (1859) 28 LJ Ch 593   7.11

Gee (Deceased), Re; *sub nom* Wood v Staples [1948] Ch 284; [1948] 1 All ER
   498; [1948] LJR 1400, ChD   6.8
Galmerrow Securities Ltd v National Westminster Bank plc (1993) unreported,
   20 December   3.55

Harries v Church Commissioners for England; *sub nom* Lord Bishop of Oxford
  v Church Commissioners of England [1992] 1 WLR 1241; [1993] 2 All ER
  300; (1991) 135 SJLB 180, ChD   3.17, 3.29
Hedley Byrne & Co Ltd v Heller & Partners Ltd [1964] AC 465; [1963] 3 WLR
  101; [1963] 2 All ER 575, HL   2.64
Holding and Management Ltd v Property Holding and Investment Trust plc
  [1989] 1 WLR 1313; [1990] 1 All ER 938; (1989) 21 HLR 596, CA   6.35

Keech v Sandford (1726) 2 Eq Cas Abr 741; (1726) 25 ER 223,
  (1726) Sel Cas Ch 61   3.65

Learoyd v Whiteley; *see* Whiteley, Re
Leighton v MacLeod; Worthington, Re; *see* Worthington (Deceased), Re
Lord Bishop of Oxford v Church Commissioners of England; *see* Harries v
  Church Commissioners for England

McEachern, Re (1911) 103 LT 900   7.11
Malcolm v O'Callaghan (1837) 3 May & Cr 52   6.35
Martin v City of Edinburgh District Council [1988] SLT 329; [1988] SCLR 90,
  OH   3.47
Mothew v Bristol and West Building Society; *see* Bristol and West Building
  Society v Mothew (ta Stapley & Co)
Mulligan (Deceased), Re [1998] 1 NZLR 481   3.54

National Trustees Co of Australia Ltd v General Finance Co of Australia Ltd
  [1905] AC 373   3.51
Nestlé v National Westminster Bank plc (No 2) [2000] WTLR 795, ChD   3.30, 3.54
Nestlé v National Westminster Bank plc (No 2) [1993] 1 WLR 1260; [1994] 1
  All ER 118; (1992) *The Times*, 11 May, CA   3.30, 3.47, 3.54
Nocton v Lord Ashburton [1914] AC 932; [1914–15] All ER Rep 45, HL   3.47

O'Sullivan v Management Agency and Music Ltd [1985] QB 428; [1984] 3
  WLR 448; [1985] 3 All ER 351, CA   6.6
Ovey v Ovey [1900] 2 Ch 524, ChD   3.61

Peel's Settled Estates, Re [1910] 1 Ch 389, ChD   4.8
Perrins v Bellamy [1899] 1 Ch 797, CA   1.1
Phipps v Boardman; *see* Boardman v Phipps
Photo Production Ltd v Securicor Transport Ltd [1980] AC 827; [1980] 2 WLR
  283; [1980] 1 All ER 556, HL   2.41
Pimms Ltd v Tallow Chandlers in the City of London [1964] 2 QB 547;
  [1964] 2 WLR 1129; [1964] 2 All ER 145, CA   3.39
Pooley, Re (1888) 40 Ch D 1   6.9

Power's Will Trusts, Re; *sub nom* Public Trustee v Hastings [1947] Ch 572;
   [1947] 2 All ER 282; (1947) 111 JP 245, ChD   4.2, 4.5
Public Trustee v Hastings; *see* Power's Will Trusts, Re

Saunders v Vautier (1841) 4 Beav 115   2.66, 7.7
Shaw v Cates [1909] 1 Ch 389, ChD   3.48
Sir Robert Peel's Settled Estates, Re; *see* Peel's Settled Estates, Re

Robinson v Pett (1734) 3 P Wms 249   6.5

Sherwood, Re (1840) 3 Beav 338   6.6
Speight, Re; *sub nom* Speight v Gaunt (1883) 9 App Cas 1; (1883) LR 22 Ch D
   727, CA   2.59, 3.51
Stafford v Fiddon (1857) 23 Beav 386   2.12

Target Holdings Ltd v Redferns (No 1) [1994] 1 WLR 1089; [1994] 2 All ER
   337, CA   2.66, 3.47

Vickery, Re; *sub nom* Vickery v Stephens [1931] 1 Ch 572, ChD   2.69

Wakeman, Re [1945] Ch 177, ChD   4.9
Waterman's Will Trusts, Re [1952] 2 All ER 1054   2.8, 2.52, 3.51
Webb v Jonas (1888) 39 Ch D 660   4.16
Whiteley, Re; *sub nom* Whiteley v Learoyd (1886) LR 33 Ch D 347, CA   2.49, 2.50,
                                                                                 3.54
Whiteley, Re; *sub nom* Learoyd v Whiteley (1887) LR 12 App Cas 727, HL   3.54
Wight v Olswang (No 2) [2000] WTLR 783; [2000] Lloyd's Rep PN 662;
   (2000) *The Times*, April 18, ChD   2.64
Wood v Staples; *see* Gee (Deceased), Re
Worby v Rosser [2000] PNLR 140; [1999] Lloyd's Rep PN 972; (1999) *The
   Times*, 9 June, CA   5.29
Worthington (Deceased), Re; *sub nom* Leighton v MacLeod; Worthington, Re
   [1954] 1 WLR 526; [1954] 1 All ER 677, ChD   6.6
Wragg, Re; *sub nom* Wragg v Palmer [1919] 2 Ch 58, ChD   3.15

X v A [2000] 1 All ER 490; (2000) 1 WTLR 11; (1999) *The Times*, October 6,
   Ch D   3.54, 6.35
X (Minors) v Bedfordshire County Council [1995] 2 AC 633; [1995] 2 FLR
   276; [1995] Fam Law 537, HL   2.64

TABLE OF STATUTES

References are to paragraph numbers and Appendix numbers.

Administration of Estates Act
  1925 — App I
  s 34 — 1.21
    (2) — 6.17
    (3) — 6.10, 6.30
Administration of Justice Act
  1982 — App I
Administration of Justice Act
  1985 — App I
  s 9 — 5.37
Agricultural Marketing Act
  1958 — App I
Agriculture Act 1967 — App I

Banking Act 1987 — 6.26, App I
Betting, Gaming and Lotteries
  Act 1963 — App I

Cathedrals Measure 1963
  (No 2) — 1.30, App 1
Cathedrals Measure 1999
  (No 1) — App 1
Cereals Marketing Act 1965 — 1.31, App I
Charities Act 1993 — 1.28, 3.62, 4.27, App I
  ss 24, 25 — 3.62, 4.27
  s 35 — 6.22
  ss 70, 71 — 1.28
  s 86 — 1.28
Church Funds Investment
  Measure 1958 (No 1) — 1.30, App I
Church of England (Pensions)
  Measure 1988 (No 4) — App I
Clergy Pensions Measure 1961
  (No 3) — 1.30, App I

Diocesan Stipends Funds
  Measure 1953 (No 2) — App I
Duchy of Cornwall
  Management Act 1893 — App I

Duchy of Cornwall
  Management Act 1982 — App I
Duchy of Lancaster Act 1920 — App I
  s 20 — 1.28

Ecclesiastical Dilapidations
  Measure 1923 (No 3) — App I

Financial Services Act 1986 — 3.36, App I
  s 78 — 4.27
  s 81 — 3.62
Fisheries Act 1981 — App I

Horticulture Act 1960 — 1.31, App I
House of Commons Members'
  Fund Act 1962 — App I

Insolvency Act 1986 — 6.30, App I
Interpretation Act 1978 — 3.13, 4.15
Income and Corporation Taxes
  Act 1988 — App I
  s 840 — 5.37

Judicial Trustees Act 1896 — 6.6
  s 1(5) — 6.6

Land Registration Act 1925 — App I
Law of Property Act 1925 — App I
  s 205 — 4.15
Law of Property (Amendment)
  Act 1926
  s 3 — 6.22
Licensing (Alcohol Education
  and Research) Act 1981 — App I

Ministers of the Crown Act
  1975 — App I

National Heritage Act 1980   App I

Pastoral Measure 1983 (No 1)   App I
Pensions Act 1995   App I
    s 20   6.6, 6.20
    s 31(4)   3.41
    s 32(3)   3.41
    s 34   3.28, 3.62
        (1)   3.12, 4.4
Pension Schemes Act 1993   App I
Places of Worship Sites Act
    1873   App I
Policyholders' Protection Act
    1975   App I
Public Trustee Act 1906   5.35, 6.20,
                                    App I
    s 4   5.5, 6.6, 6.20
        (3)   6.22
    s 9   6.6

Recognition of Trusts Act 1987   1.13,
                                     4.17
Regimental Charitable Funds
    Act 1935   1.31, App I
Repair of Benefice Buildings
    Measure 1972 (No 2)   App I

Settled Land Act 1925   1.29, 4.3, 4.6–
                          4.10, 4.27, 4.31,
                          4.32, 4.35, 4.37,
                          5.8, 7.8, App I
    s 73   4.29
        (1)   4.8
    s 75   4.34
        (2)   4.8, 4.31
        (4)   4.8, 4.32, 4.31
        (4A)   4.31
        (4B), (4C)   4.32
    s 75A   4.35
        (1)   4.35
        (2)–(5)   4.36
    s 107(1A)(a), (c), (d)   2.37
Solicitors' Act 1974   App I

Technical and Industrial
    Institutions Act 1892   App I

Trustee Act 1893   App I
    s 1   1.28
Trustee Act 1925   1.1, 1.29, 2.26,
                          2.29, 2.58, 3.19,
                          3.47, 5.4, 5.6,
                          5.12, 6.22, App I
    s 6   3.19
    s 7(1)   5.5, 5.38
    s 8   3.21
    s 9   3.22
    s 10(2)   4.35
    s 15   1.24, 2.10, 2.24,
                          2.26, 2.29
        (a)–(f)   2.24
    s 19   1.22, 2.27, 7.1,
                          7.3, 7.4, 7.6–7.9
        (1)   7.3
            (a), (b)   7.6
        (2)   7.3
            (a), (b)   7.7
        (3)(a), (b)   7.7
        (5)   7.6
    s 21   5.5
    s 22(1), (3)   1.24, 2.10, 2.28
    s 23   2.23, 2.26, 2.29,
                          2.59, 2.69
        (1)   2.2, 2.55, 5.3
        (2)   5.3
        (3)   2.2, 2.55, 5.3
            (a)   5.3
            (c)   5.3
    s 30   2.2, 2.23, 2.55, 2.59
    s 42   6.6
    s 68(17)   6.22
Trustee Act 2000   1.1, 1.2, 1.4, 1.6,
                          1.7, 1.9, 1.10–1.14,
                          1.16, 1.21, 1.22,
                          1.26–1.28, 1.32–1.34,
                          2.3, 2.4, 2.10, 2.16,
                          2.18, 2.19, 2.25,
                          2.29–2.31, 2.34–2.38,
                          2.40, 2.47, 2.50–2.53,
                          2.55, 2.60–2.64,
                          2.67–2.70, 2.72,
                          2.73, 3.4, 3.5, 3.10,
                          3.13, 3.15, 3.18,
                          3.21, 3.22, 3.29,
                          3.38, 3.40, 3.43,
                          3.45, 3.49, 3.50,

Trustee Act 2000 – *cont*	3.54–3.56,	(1)	1.15, 2.45, 3.23
	3.58,	(2)	3.25, 3.33
	3.60–3.66, 4.1,	(3) (a)	1.15, 3.26
	4.3, 4.4, 4.10, 4.13,	(b)	1.15, 3.26, 3.30, 3.31
	4.14–4.16, 4.25–4.27,	ss 4–7	3.2
	4.30–4.35, 5.1–5.3,	s 5	1.15, 1.24, 2.10,
	5.6–5.8, 5.10,		2.13, 2.14, 2.16,
	5.15–5.18, 5.22,		3.14, 3.37, 3.45,
	5.26, 5.29, 5.30,		3.46, 3.49, 3.50,
	5.35, 5.41, 5.44,		4.36, 5.26, 5.28
	5.46, 5.48, 5.50,	(1)	1.15, 3.32
	6.1, 6.3, 6.5–6.8,	(2)	3.33
	6.10–6.12, 6.16,	(3)	3.32, 3.38, 3.40
	6.18, 6.20, 6.22,	(4)	1.15, 3.32, 3.41
	6.28, 6.30, 6.31,	s 6	3.56
	6.35, 6.37, 6.42,	(1) (b)	3.24??, 3.58
	6.43, 7.2, 7.3,	(4)	3.41
	7.7, 7.8, 7.11,	s 7	1.16
	7.14, App I, App III	(1)	1.16, 3.62
Pt I	2.1, 2.2	(2)	3.58, 3.59
Pt II	1.14, 1.17, 3.12, 3.62	(3)	1.16, 3.61, 3.62
Pt III	1.17, 1.18, 3.12, 3.62, 4.3,	s 8	1.14, 2.10, 2.16,
	4.25–4.29, 4.37		3.13, 4.11–4.13, 4.15, 4.17,
Pt IV	1.19, 5.7, 5.48,		4.22, 4.24–4.26, 4.29,
	6.24, 6.33, 6.36, 6.38		App III
Pt VI	7.1	(1) (a)–(c)	1.17
s 1	1.13, 1.23, 2.3,	(2)	4.15
	2.34, 3.44, App III	(a)	1.17
(1)	1.25, 2.3, 2.6, 2.7, 2.25, 2.32,	(3)	1.17, 4.21, 4.22
	2.50, 2.52, 2.63, 3.51	s 9(a)	1.18, 4.25
(a)	2.3, 2.4, 2.5–2.7, 2.39, 2.51,	(b)	1.18, 4.26
	3.52, 3.53, App III	s 10(1)	4.29
(b)	2.3, 2.4, 2.5–2.7, 2.51, 2.52,	(a), (b)	4.27
	3.53, App III	(2)	4.28
(2)	2.63	s 11	1.19, 4.32, 5.8,
s 3	2.13, 3.2, 3.46,		5.9, 5.26, 5.34,
	3.49, 3.64, 4.11, 5.26		5.40, 7.7
(1)	3.11, 3.12, 3.23	(1)	5.9, 5.34
(2)	1.14, 3.11	(2)	5.11
(3)	1.14, 3.13, 4.15	(a)–(d)	5.10
(4)	3.20	(3)	5.13, 6.39
(a)	3.20	(a)–(d)	5.13
(5)	3.20	(c)	5.14
(6)	3.20	(4)	5.14
ss 3–7	1.14, 3.5	(a), (b)	5.14
s 4	1.24, 2.10, 2.13,	s 12(2)–(4)	5.16
	2.14, 2.16, 3.14, 3.46, 3.49,	s 13	5.27, 5.28–5.32, 5.34
	3.50,	(1)	5.26–5.28, 5.32, 5.33
	5.26, 5.28, 5.32	(2)	5.26

Trustee Act 2000 – *cont*
s 13(4), (5)	5.34
ss 13–15	5.8
s 14	1.20, 5.17, 5.27, 5.39
(1)	5.17
(2)	5.18
(3)(a)–(c)	5.18
s 15	2.71, 5.42, 5.46, App III
(1)	5.25
(2)	5.17
(a)	2.20, 5.25
(b)(i), (ii)	5.25
(3), (4)	5.25, 5.42
(5)	5.25
s 16	5.40
(1)(a), (b)	5.35
(2), (3)	5.35
s 17	5.36, 5.40
(1)–(4)	5.36
s 18	1.19, 5.38, 5.40, 5.49
(1), (3), (4)	5.38
s 19	5.37
(2)(a)–(c)	5.37
(5)–(7)	5.37
s 20	5.39
(2), (3)	5.39
s 21	3.56, 5.40
ss 21–23	5.8
s 22	1.20, 2.10, 2.19, 2.22, 2.56–2.58, 5.41, 5.43, 5.44
(1)	5.42
(a)	2.28, 5.40
(b)	2.20, 2.28, 5.40
(c)	2.28, 5.40
(d)	2.28
(2)(a)–(c)	5.42
(3)	2.28, 5.42
s 23	1.20, 2.22, 2.57, 2.58, 5.43, 5.44
(1)	2.56, 2.57, 2.59, 5.44
(a), (b)	5.44
(4)	5.40
s 24	5.46
s 25(1)	5.47
(2)	5.38
s 26(a)	5.7
(b)	5.7
s 27	5.7

s 28	6.13, 6.11, 6.19, 6.30
(1)	6.13, 6.18
(a)	6.13
(2)	6.13, 6.14
(3)	6.15
(4)	6.13, 6.17
(5)	6.23, 6.28
(a), (b)	6.28
(6)	6.14
s 29	2.8, 6.20, 6.30, App III
(1)	6.11, 6.21
(2)	6.23
(2) *et seq*	6.11
(3)	6.21, 6.23, 6.25, 6.26
(4)	6.21, 6.23
(5)	6.20
(6)	5.23, 6.24
ss 29–32	5.17, 5.39
s 30	6.11
(1)	6.33
(2)	5.23, 6.33
(3)	6.34
(4)	6.34
s 31(1)	6.35
(2)	5.24, 6.36
s 32	5.8, 6.11, 6.38
(1)	6.38
(2)(a), (b)	5.20, 6.40
(3)	5.20, 6.41
s 33(1)	6.16, 6.20, 6.37, 6.42
(2)	6.19
s 34	2.27, 7.6
(3)	7.8
s 35	2.18
(1)	2.9, 2.34
(2)(b), (c)	4.13
(3)	6.30
(4)	6.31
s 36(2)	1.13
(3)	3.12, 3.62, 4. 27
s 37	3.62, 4.27
s 38	3.62, 4.27
s 39(1)	6.22
s 40	3.22
s 41	3.63
Sch 1	1.23, 2.10, 2.16, 2.17, 2.21, 2.30, 2.35, 2.56, 2.63, 2.73
para 1	2.11, 2.34, 3.46, 3.50

Trustee Act 2000 – *cont*
Sch 1, para 1(a)   2.11, 2.13
    (b)   2.13
    para 2   2.15, 2.34
    (a)   2.16, 4.22
    (b)   1.13, 2.16, 4.22
    (c)   4.22
    para 3   1.20, 2.19, 2.34, 2.56,
    6.40
    (1)   5.17
    (a)   2.19, 2.56
    (b)   2.19, 2.56
    (c)   2.19, 2.56
    (d)   1.13, 2.19, 2.56
    (e)   2.19, 2.56, 2.57,
    5.43
    (2)(a), (b)   2.20
    para 4   2.34, 7.8, 7.9
    (a)   2.24
Sch 1, para 4(b)   1.13, 2.24
    para 5   2.27, 2.34, 4.23, 7.9
    para 6   2.34
    (a), (b)   2.28
    para 7   1.8, 1.13, 2.39, 2.46,
    2.47
Sch 2   1.28, 1.31, 3.63
    para 1(3)(a)   3.22
    paras 5–15   4.30
    para 8   4.34
    (1), (2)   4.31
    (3)   4.34
    para 9   4.35
    para 17   2.37, 5.8
    para 20   2.25
    paras 23, 24   2.55, 2.59
Sch 3, para 2   3.21
    para 3   3.22
    para 7   4.15
Sch 4   2.23
Trustee Delegation Act 1999   5.2

Trustee Investments Act 1961   1.1, 1.5,
    1.14, 1.28, 1.32,
    3.1, 3.6–3.8, 3.10,
    3.14, 3.19, 3.23,
    3.24, 3.33, 3.36,
    3.37, 3.40–3.42,
    3.56–3.61, 4.4,
    4.10, 4.15, App I
s 1(3)   3.58
s 2   3.10
s 3(1)   3.9
s 6(1)   3.23, 4.20
    (a)   3.30, 3.56, 3.61
    (b)   3.56
    (5)   3.36
Sch 1   3.7
Sch 1, Pt I   3.7, 3.34
    Pt II   3.7, 3.19, 3.34
    para 13   4.4
Sch 2, para 1   3.9
Trusts of Land and
    Appointment of Trustees
    Act 1996   1.29, 4.6–4.10,
    4.31, 7.3, 7.4,
    7.8, App I
s 1   4.9
s 2   4.29
    (1)   4.7
    (4)   4.8
s 6   4.24
    (1)   4.9, 7.4
    (3), (4)   4.9, 4.12
    (5)   4.24
s 17(1)   4.9

Universities and College Estates
    Act 1925   4.27, 4.37

Wills Act 1837
    s 15   1.21, 6.9, 6.17

TABLE OF STATUTORY INSTRUMENTS

References are to paragraph numbers.

Occupational Pension Schemes (Investment and Assignment, Forfeiture,
    Bankruptcy etc) Amendment Regulations 1999, SI 1999/1849   3.29

Public Trustee (Custodian Trustee) Rules 1975, SI 1975/1189   6.22
Trustee Investments (Additional Powers) Order No 2 1994, SI 1994/1908   3.10
Trustee Investments (Division of Trust Fund) Order 1996, SI 1996/845   3.8

TABLE OF INTERNATIONAL LEGISLATION

References are to paragraph numbers.

Hague Convention on the Law Applicable to Trusts and on their
  Recognition   1.13, 4.17, 4.18

TABLE OF ABBREVIATIONS

the Act	Trustee Act 2000
the Report or Law Com No 260	'Trustees' Powers and Duties' (Report No 260 by the Law Commission)
1925 Act	Trustee Act 1925
STEP	Society of Trust and Estate Practitioners
1961 Act	Trustee Investments Act 1961
1996 Act	Trusts of Land and Appointment of Trustees Act 1996

Chapter 1

INTRODUCTION AND BACKGROUND

'The main duty of a trustee is to commit judicious breaches of trust.'[1]

INTRODUCTION

1.1 Whether or not Sir Nathaniel Lindley MR was providing an accurate description of the role of trustees when he uttered the words quoted above over 100 years ago is open to debate. What is certain is that the law relating to the powers and duties of trustees has evolved considerably in the last century, the most notable developments being the passing of the Trustee Act 1925 and the Trustee Investments Act 1961. The Trustee Act 2000 ('the Act') is a further stage in that evolutionary process, being an attempt by Parliament to give trustees the requisite powers to administer trusts effectively in the present day.

THE BACKGROUND TO THE LEGISLATION

The Law Commission

1.2 The Act has come into being almost entirely due to the efforts of the Law Commission. In its report No 260[2] ('the Report'), the Law Commission[3] identified the need for reform of the powers given to, and the duties imposed upon trustees. In the introduction to the Report, the following comment is made[4]:

'... The law governing the powers and duties of trustees has not kept pace with the evolving economic and social nature of trusts – indeed the default powers which trustees have under the present law are generally regarded as seriously restrictive.'

1.3 The Report cites the following as the main reasons for trustees' default powers having become outdated:

---

1   Per Sir Nathaniel Lindley MR in *Perrins v Bellamy* [1899] 1 Ch 797 at 798 attributing the remark to Selwyn LJ.
2   'Trustees Powers and Duties' Law Com No 260 (HMSO, July 1999). The original draft of the Bill was contained in an appendix to the report.
3   The Report was actually a joint report of the Law Commission and the Scottish Law Commission, and therefore also made recommendations in respect of Scots law. The Trustee Act 2000 (and therefore this book) deal only with the position in England and Wales.
4   The Report, para 1.1.

'(1) the introduction in 1995 of five-day rolling settlement for dealings in shares and securities listed on the London Stock Exchange;

(2) the introduction in 1996 of dematerialised holding and transfer of title to shares and securities listed on the London Stock Exchange under the CREST system;

(3) the use of similar computerised clearing systems in other markets in which trustees may wish to invest; and

(4) the widespread employment of discretionary fund managers to enable full advantage to be taken of the increasingly complex range of investment opportunities.'[5]

1.4 Thus the changes introduced by the Act represent an attempt to improve the default powers given to trustees, so that they are able to take full advantage of the breadth of investment opportunities and working practices available in the modern world.

THE LAW COMMISSION'S PRINCIPAL RECOMMENDATIONS

1.5 The principal recommendations of the Law Commission are summarised at para 1.33 of the Report. They are as follows.

(1) Insofar as it governs the powers of investment of trustees in England and Wales and in Scotland, the Trustee Investments Act 1961 should be repealed and replaced with a new statutory provision giving trustees power to make an investment of any kind as if they were absolutely (or beneficially) entitled to the assets of the trust. Trustees should also have power to acquire land on behalf of the trust.

(2) In England and Wales, trustees:
    (a) should have power to delegate to agents their powers to administer the trust (other than powers to appoint or dismiss trustees) including their powers of investment and management; but
    (b) should have no authority to delegate their powers to distribute the income or capital of the trust for the benefit of its objects.

(3) In England and Wales, the trustees should have a power:
    (a) to vest trust assets in the name of a nominee; and
    (b) to deposit trust documents or trust property with a custodian for safe keeping;

provided that such person acts as a nominee or custodian in the course of its business.

---

5   The Report, para 1.2.

(4) All trustees in England and Wales should have the same power to insure the trust property as they would if they were the absolute owners of it.

(5) In England and Wales, trustees should have power to authorise one (or more) of their number to charge for his or her services on behalf of the trust if he or she is acting in a professional capacity.

(6) In addition to complying with specific conditions which apply to the exercise of some of the powers proposed, a trustee in England and Wales should, when exercising any of those powers, act with such care and skill as is reasonable in the circumstances, having regard in particular to any special knowledge or experience that he or she has, or holds him or herself out as having, and if he or she acts as trustee in the course of a business or profession, to any special knowledge that it is reasonable to expect of a person acting in the course of that kind of business or profession.

1.6   The recommendations listed above were all incorporated into the Law Commission's draft Trustee Bill which, with some relatively minor alterations, has become the Trustee Act 2000 as enacted by Parliament.

PARLIAMENT

1.7   The Act had an extremely smooth (if lengthy) passage through both Houses of Parliament. Whilst certain amendments were proposed in both the Lords and the Commons, only those put forward by the Lord Chancellor's Department found their way into the Act. These amendments were essentially a 'tidying up' exercise and did very little of substance other than bring compounding of liabilities, reversionary interests, valuation and audit within the scope of the statutory duty of care[6].

1.8   The only issue raised in debate which might be described as contentious was the question of exclusion clauses. On the second reading of the Bill in the Lords, objection was taken to para 7 of Sch 1, which permits the exclusion of the statutory duty of care[7]. In response to those objections[8], the Lord Chancellor undertook to refer the issue of trustee exemption clauses (presumably including issues relating to para 7 of Sch 1 to the Act) to the Law Commission for its consideration[9].

---

6   See Chapter 2 below.
7   See para **2.39**.
8   Raised by Lord Goodhart QC. See Hansard, 14 April 2000, at para 383.
9   See Hansard, 14 April 2000, at para 393, per Lord Irvine of Lairg LC.

1.9   The Act finally passed through its third reading and report stages in the Commons on 8 November 2000, and received Royal Assent on 23 November 2000. A full table of the debates concerning the Act, and the references to Hansard may be found at Appendix II. The Act's commencement date is 1 February 2001.

APPLICATION AND OUTLINE OF THE ACT

The application of the Act

1.10   The best summary of the scope of the Act is perhaps that given by the Law Commission in relation to its report[10], namely: '... *what* investments trustees should be permitted to make in the absence of express authority in the instrument creating the trust, and also ... *how* they should be able to achieve the effective administration of a trust'.

1.11   It was therefore the Law Commission's intention that the Act should be very wide, governing all types of trust wherever possible[11]. It was, however, recognised that due to the special regimes applying to certain types of trusts (most notably pension trusts and charitable trusts) there are certain situations where the Act's provisions should not apply so as not to interfere with the special treatment afforded to such trusts.

1.12   As many modern trust instruments contain very wide powers for trustees, it may be that the trustees of such trusts will not need to rely upon their new powers under the Act. However, where the instrument is not drafted in such wide terms; where the trust instrument is silent as to the trustees' powers (as is the case with many will trusts); and where the trust is created either by implication or by statute, the Act will be of particular importance, as it will define the scope of trustees' powers.

1.13   The new statutory duty of care created by s 1 of the Act[12] will, however, have a wider application. The duty applies (unless otherwise excluded[13]) not only to the exercise by trustees of the various powers given to them by virtue of the Act, but also where the trustee is exercising similar powers conferred by the trust instrument[14]. However, it does not apply to the exercise of certain powers by trustees of occupational pension schemes[15]. The Act does not set out what the position is as regards UK resident trustees of non-resident trusts. For example, a trust may have three trustees, one of

---

10   The Report, para 1.13 (emphasis added).
11   Ibid, para 1.20.
12   See Chapter 2 below.
13   In accordance with Sch 1, para 7 to the Act.
14   See, for example, Sch 1, paras 2(b) and 3(1)(d) and 4(b) to the Act.
15   Trustee Act 2000, s 36(2).

whom is resident in the UK, the other two being resident in, say, Jersey. Does the UK resident trustee have the powers and duties created by the Act? The answer will depend upon the proper law of the trust, which determines the nature and extent of beneficiaries' rights. The proper law will often be stated explicitly in the trust instrument itself, otherwise it will be determined in accordance with conflict of laws principles[16]. Where English law is the proper law of the trusts, all of the trustees will be subject to the powers and duties under the Act save insofar as they have been restricted in accordance with it.

Trustees' investment powers[17]

1.14 Part II of the Act (ss 3–7) contains provisions which extend the powers of trustees in relation to the investment of trust assets, replacing the previous regime contained in the Trustee Investments Act 1961. The most important change is that the Act now enables trustees to make investments as if they were absolutely entitled to the assets comprised in the trust, rather than having the power only to deal in certain specified investments. The new power is known as 'the general power of investment'[18] and applies only insofar as no contrary intention is expressed in the trust instrument. It should be noted, however, that s 3(3) of the Act provides that the general power of investment does not permit trustees to make any investment in land save for 'loans secured on land'[19].

1.15 When exercising the general power of investment, trustees are required by s 4(1) of the Act to have regard to the 'standard investment criteria'[20]. In addition, s 5 requires trustees to obtain and consider proper advice[21] about the way in which the general power of investment should be exercised in light of the standard investment criteria. This need not be done

---

16   In particular, the Hague Convention on the Law Applicable to Trusts and on their Recognition. This Convention was implemented in the UK by the Recognition of Trusts Act 1987. For a full commentary on the substance of the Convention and the rules governing questions of a trust's 'proper law', see DJ Hayton: *Underhill and Hayton, Law of Trusts and Trustees*, 15th edn (Butterworths) at p 939.

17   See further Chapter 3 below.

18   Trustee Act 2000, s 3(2).

19   However, a wider power of investment in land is contained within s 8. See **1.17** and Chapter 4 below.

20   Which are defined by s 4(3) of the Act as being: '(a) the suitability to the trust of investments of the same kind as any particular investment proposed to be made or retained and of that particular investment as an investment of that kind, and (b) the need for diversification of investments of the trust, in so far as is appropriate to the circumstances of the trust'. See paras **3.23** *et seq*.

21   Defined by s 5(4) of the Act as: '... the advice of a person who is reasonably believed by the trustee to be qualified to give it by his ability and practical experience of financial and other matters relating to the proposed investment'.

by a trustee where he 'reasonably concludes that in all the circumstances it is unnecessary or inappropriate to do so'[22].

1.16   By s 7, the general power of investment is conferred in addition to those powers already conferred upon trustees otherwise than by the Act, but subject to any restrictions contained in the trust instrument. The power is not conferred on trustees who, immediately prior to commencement of the Act, had 'special statutory powers of investment'[23]. Such powers are defined[24] as being a power which is conferred by an enactment or subordinate legislation on trustees of a particular trust or type of trust.

Acquisition of land [25]

1.17   Whilst the general power of investment given to trustees by Part II of the Act does not give them the power to acquire land, separate powers in relation to the acquisition of land are given to trustees by Part III of the Act. The new powers are extensive, and enable trustees to buy freehold or leasehold land[26] in the UK:

(1)   as an investment[27];
(2)   for occupation by a beneficiary[28]; or
(3)   for any other reason[29].

In relation to land, a trustee is given[30] all the powers of an absolute owner.

1.18   The powers conferred upon trustees by Part III are in addition to any conferred under the trust deed[31], but are subject to any restrictions or exclusions imposed by the trust deed, or any enactment or provision of subordinate legislation[32] and are not given to certain classes of trustees[33].

Agents, custodians and nominees[34]

1.19   Part IV of the Act introduces a new regime for the appointment of agents, custodians and nominees by trustees. Under the new provisions, trustees collectively may authorise an agent to carry out any of their

---

22   Trustee Act 2000, s 5(1).
23   Ibid, s 7(1).
24   Ibid, s 7(3).
25   See further Chapter 4 below.
26   Defined by s 8(2)(a) as a legal estate in land.
27   Section 8(1)(a).
28   Section 8(1)(b).
29   Section 8(1)(c).
30   By s 8(3).
31   Section 9(a).
32   Section 9(b).
33   See para **4.27**.
34   See further Chapter 5 below.

'delegable functions'[35]. In addition, trustees are given wide powers to use custodians and nominees to hold trust property; indeed, in certain circumstances, trustees are under a duty to deposit some types of assets with custodians[36].

1.20 Trustees are restricted as to the terms upon which they may appoint agents, custodians or nominees, with certain terms such as exclusion clauses and terms permitting an agent to act in situations where a conflict of interests may arise only being permissible where they are 'reasonably necessary'[37]. Most importantly, perhaps, trustees are under a duty to review the activities of their agents, custodians and nominees[38]. Trustees are subject to the new statutory duty of care when appointing agents, custodians or nominees, and also when reviewing their activities[39], but otherwise are not liable for any default of the agent, custodian or nominee[40].

Remuneration[41]

1.21 The Act also reforms the law concerning the entitlement of trustees to remuneration for their services, by enabling trust corporations to charge 'reasonable remuneration' for the services they provide to their trusts, and permitting other professional trustees (although not charitable or sole trustees) to charge reasonable remuneration if each of the other trustees agrees in writing. Importantly for many trustees, where trusts include charging provisions the Act enables professional trustees to charge for services which a lay trustee could have performed. The issue of charging by charitable trustees will be dealt with by way of regulations to be produced by the Secretary of State after further consultation. The Act also reforms the rule which treats the remuneration which a trustee may receive under a charging clause as a gift for the purposes of s 15 of the Wills Act 1837[42] and s 34 of the Administration of Estates Act 1925[43].

Insurance[44]

1.22 The Act replaces the tortuous provisions of s 19 of the Trustee Act 1925 giving trustees wide powers to insure trust property, and the ability to pay for the premiums out of the capital or income of the trust fund. Where

---

35   As defined by s 11.
36   Trustee Act 2000, s 18.
37   Ibid, s 14.
38   Ibid, s 22.
39   Ibid, Sch 1, para 3.
40   Ibid, s 23.
41   See further Chapter 6 below.
42   Rendering a charging clause in favour of a trustee who witnesses the will invalid.
43   Which does not treat remuneration under a charging clause as a debt of the estate.
44   See further Chapter 7 below.

the trust is a bare trust, the power to insure is subject to the direction of the beneficiaries as to whether assets should be insured and/or on what terms. Further, the exercise of the power is subject to the statutory duty of care. The provisions relating to insurance apply to all trusts, whenever created.

The statutory duty of care[45]

1.23 Section 1 imposes a statutory duty of care upon trustees in the circumstances set out in Sch 1 to the Act. Interestingly, the duty of care applies only in those specified situations and not otherwise. Accordingly, any act which involves a failure by a trustee to exercise reasonable care and skill, but is not mentioned in Sch 1, will be actionable not under the new provisions but under the pre-existing law.

1.24 The situations in which the statutory duty of care applies are as follows:

(a) when exercising the general power of investment (or any other power of investment howsoever conferred) and/or when carrying out the duties under ss 4 and 5;

(b) when acquiring land or exercising any power in connection with land;

(c) when entering into arrangements for the appointment of agents, custodians or nominees and carrying out the reviewing duties;

(d) when exercising the powers under s 15 of the Trustee Act 1925, or any other similar power to compound liabilities;

(e) when exercising powers of insurance; and

(f) when exercising the powers under s 22(1) or (3) of the Trustee Act 1925, or other similar powers.

The duty of care may also be excluded by a settlor incorporating words to that effect in the trust deed.

1.25 The standard of care expected of trustees is that which is 'reasonable in the circumstances' taking into account all the relevant circumstances, but particularly the subjective and objective factors set out in s 1(1) of the Act.

COMMENCEMENT OF THE ACT

1.26 At the time of going to print, no date had been announced for the commencement of the Act. The authors have, however, been informed (albeit informally) by the Lord Chancellor's Department that the intention is for the Act to be brought into force by statutory instrument on a date approximately 2 months after Royal Assent. Accordingly, commencement should be expected on or around 1 February 2001.

---

45   See further Chapter 2.

1.27 It is important to note, however, that most of the provisions contained in the Act will apply to trusts created prior to the commencement of the Act, and as a consequence it will be necessary for all trustees to take account of the contents of the Act, not just the trustees of post-Act trusts.

SOME CONSEQUENTIAL AND MINOR AMENDMENTS

1.28 The Act amends a number of Acts[46]. The two main ones are the Trustee Investments Act 1961 which is almost wholly repealed[47] and the Charities Act 1993[48]. There is a large number of other Acts which are amended to enable funds and monies arising to be invested in accordance with the general power of investment conferred by the new Act. For example, funds of the Duchy of Lancaster which under s 1 of the Duchy of Lancaster Act 1920 could be invested only in accordance with s 1 of the Trustee Act 1893, are, after the commencement of the Act, capable of being invested in accordance with the general power of investment.

1.29 There are also extensive amendments made to the Settled Land Act 1925, the Trustee Act 1925, and to the recent Trusts of Land and Appointment of Trustees Act 1996 which are dealt with in Chapter 4 of this book.

1.30 A number of ecclesiastical measures have also been amended by the Act. These include the Clergy Pensions Measure 1961, the Cathedrals Measure 1963 and the Church Funds Investment Measure 1958. The effect of the amendments is to enable the various bodies able to invest funds under these measures to have the benefit of the general power of investment. The other powers and duties do not, however, apply.

1.31 A number of other enactments in a variety of fields have been amended so as to permit bodies to use the general power of investment without having the other powers and duties of trustees. Examples include the Cereals Marketing Act 1965, the Horticulture Act 1960 and the Regimental Charitable Funds Act 1935. Full details of the repeals and amendments may be found in Sch 2 to that Act.

---

46   See Sch 2.
47   As to which, see Chapter 3 below.
48   Sections 70 and 71 which provided for regulations to relax the wider range investments in which charity trustees could invest have been repealed, being no longer necessary, and there are consequential amendments to s 86 of the Act as a result of that.

AUTHORS' VIEW OF THE ACT

1.32   The Act contains many reforms which will enable trusts relying upon the statutory default powers to be an effective medium for holding property in the 21st century. In particular, the long-overdue changes to the investment powers of trusts should be welcomed, as they permit trustees to purchase investments which individuals are commonly using, but which the overly restrictive Trustee Investments Act 1961 prevented trustees from taking advantage of. Similarly, the introduction of wider delegation powers is a positive development in trust law, as trustees are now able to employ investment managers and similar professionals in order to maximise trust investment returns.

1.33   However, there are numerous flaws in the Act. Many very obvious questions are left unanswered, perhaps the most crucial being that of how a beneficiary is to bring an action for breach of the statutory duty of care. It is in the context of that statutory duty in which the Act's deficiencies are most obvious, with the limited scope of the duty creating the potential for absurdities such as a trustee who fails to insure trust property at all being judged by a different standard of care to one who insures trust property, but fails to cover the appropriate risks[49].

1.34   In addition, the drafting of the Act leaves something to be desired in certain contexts. For example, no definitions of 'trustee', 'land' or 'investment' are provided. This may well cause disputes in the future, disputes which could so easily have been avoided had the time and care been taken to deal with these and the other points of criticism raised in this book.

1.35   Overall, however, this is a good Act, and therefore one which should be welcomed by those who have to deal with the administration of trusts and trust law generally. However, it must be hoped that it forms part of a wider programme of trust reform which will also deal with issues such as trustee exemption clauses, apportionment and trustees' dealings with third parties.

---

49   See para **2.27**.

Chapter 2

THE STATUTORY DUTY OF CARE

'Thank God, I have done my duty.'[1]

INTRODUCTION

2.1 In its Report[2], the Law Commission recognised that by widening the scope of trustees' investment powers and increasing their powers of delegation, they would create the need for additional safeguards to protect the interests of beneficiaries[3]. It is for this reason that Part I of the Act introduces a new statutory duty of care.

2.2 The imposition of a duty of care upon trustees is not a new concept. It is clear that trustees owe a duty of care to beneficiaries when investing trust property, being required to take: '... such care as an ordinary prudent man would take if he were minded to make an investment for the benefit of other people for whom he felt morally bound to provide'[4]. Further, ss 23(1), (3) and 30 of the Trustee Act 1925 (the 1925 Act) imposed certain duties in relation to delegation[5]. What the new Act is intended to do is create '... a uniform duty [of care], with the same standard of care applying in respect of each of the functions to which it applie[s]'[6]. One of the aims of the creation of a uniform duty is to provide '... certainty and consistency to the standard of competence and behaviour expected of trustees'[7]. The purpose of this chapter is to consider the provisions of Part I of the Act and the extent to which the stated aim is achieved.

THE BASIC DUTY

2.3 The basic duty imposed upon trustees by the Act is contained within s 1. It requires trustees to 'exercise such care and skill as is reasonable in the circumstances'[8]. It is immediately apparent that the question of what constitutes 'reasonable care and skill' will be an issue of fact for determination in each case, taking into account all of the circumstances. Guidance

---

1   Horatio, Lord Nelson at the Battle of Trafalgar.
2   Law Com No 260.
3   Ibid, para 3.8.
4   See, for example, *Cowan v Scargill* [1985] Ch 270.
5   These sections are repealed by the Act. See **2.55**.
6   Law Com No 260, para 3.9.
7   Hansard, 14 April 2000, at para 374, per Lord Irvine of Lairg LC.
8   Trustee Act 2000, s 1(1).

as to which factors will be of particular relevance is given by s 1(1)(a) and (b) which provide that specific regard must be given to the following:

(a) any special knowledge or experience the trustee holds himself out as having; and
(b) where the trustee acts in the course of a business or profession, any special knowledge or experience it is reasonable to expect of a person acting in the course of that business or profession.

2.4   The matters listed in s 1(1)(a) and (b) create what might best be described as a 'subjective/objective test' in that para (a) is subjective, looking at the circumstances of the particular trustee in question; whereas para (b) is objective, looking to the standards which can reasonably be expected from a member of that trustee's business or profession. The first question which arises in respect of s 1(1)(b) is how wide is the definition of a 'business or profession'? It is submitted that, in the absence of any specific definitions in the Act, the terms must be given their ordinary, everyday meaning. Therefore, s 1(1)(b) will treat all solicitors, for example, as owing the same prima facie duty of care when acting as trustees, even if their expertise, experience and knowledge varies quite considerably. This is not as problematical as it may seem at first glance, as although s 1(1)(b) imposes a minimum standard which can be applied to *all* members of a particular 'business' or 'profession', it does not limit the duty of a specialist within that business or profession to that of the reasonable member of that business or profession. This is because s 1(1)(a) provides that when ascertaining the level of care and skill to be expected from *any* trustee (and not just those acting in the course of a business or profession) 'any special knowledge or experience that he has or holds himself out as having' is to be taken into account. Thus the Act quite rightly provides a mechanism for treating a high street solicitor acting as a trustee for only one client differently to a private client specialist who acts as trustee for numerous trusts.

2.5   Whilst it is clear that s 1(1)(a) will frequently be used to impose a higher duty upon 'specialist' trustees, it remains to be seen whether it can work so as to do the opposite: to reduce the standard expected under s 1(1)(b) in cases where the trustee professes to have a lack of expertise. Whilst this may appear to be an unlikely proposition, the following scenario ought to be considered: A high street solicitor is approached by a long-standing client of his to act as a trustee. The solicitor is reluctant to do so, as he does not carry out trust work and therefore has no experience or knowledge of trust administration. He informs the client of this. The client is, however, insistent and reluctantly the solicitor accepts the appointment.

2.6   In the situation described above, there are two possible ways in which s 1(1) might operate, and as a consequence two possible standards of care which might be expected from the solicitor.

(1) The first way would be to start with s 1(1)(b)[9], and thereby impose a prima facie duty to act with the care and skill of a reasonable solicitor. However, s 1(1)(a) requires a consideration of 'the special knowledge or experience the trustee has or holds himself out as having' and therefore arguably in this case, as the solicitor has held himself out to be, in effect, an amateur, the duty imposed upon him should in fact be lower than that imposed by s 1(1)(b).

(2) The alternative is to start with s 1(1)(a), and impose a low duty upon the solicitor by virtue of his personal knowledge and experience, but then to impose upon him a higher duty (ie that of the reasonable solicitor) under s 1(1)(b) as he acts as trustee in the course of his profession. Thus, no matter what the solicitor might say about his abilities, knowledge and experience in respect of trust administration, s 1(1)(b) will impose the duty owed by a reasonable solicitor upon him.

2.7 In the authors' view, the latter of the two propositions is the correct one: a person acting as a trustee in the course of his business or profession will have a minimum standard imposed upon him by s 1(1)(b). Whilst this may be considered somewhat unfair, especially where the trustee has been frank and open about his position, support for this proposition can be found. First, the guidance notes to s 1(1) state as follows: '... in the circumstances contemplated in [section] 1(1)(a) and (b) there may be an 'uplift' in the standard of care that might otherwise apply[10]'. This shows that s 1(1)(b) is intended to impose a minimum standard upon professional trustees, rather than one which can be lowered by reference to s 1(1)(a).

2.8 Secondly, it would seem that the automatically higher standard of care is a necessary *quid pro quo* of the right to remuneration under s 29 of the Act for trust corporations and those acting in a 'professional capacity' [11]. Such a position is consistent with that at common law, which always requires a higher standard of care from a trustee in receipt of remuneration from the trust than from one who was not[12].

2.9 The problems discussed above may well prove to be common. The term 'trustee' used in the act includes personal representatives[13], and therefore all solicitors who accept an appointment as executor on a professional basis will be subject to the duty of care, and will be expected to

---

9   As the solicitor is clearly acting in the course of his profession.

10   Law Com No 260, at p 97.

11   See Chapter 6 below.

12   See *Re Waterman's Will Trusts* [1952] 2 All ER 1054; *Bartlett v Barclays Bank Trust Co Ltd (No 2)* [1980] Ch 515 at 534.

13   See s 35(1) of the Act.

perform with the competence of the 'reasonable solicitor' notwithstanding any lack of trusts and estates experience on their part[14].

APPLICATION OF THE STATUTORY DUTY OF CARE

General application

2.10   Schedule 1 to the Act sets out the specific situations in which the new statutory duty of care will apply. They are as follows:

–   when a trustee is exercising the general power of investment, or any other power of investment[15];
–   when a trustee is carrying out the duties imposed by s 4 or s 5 of the Act[16];
–   when a trustee is exercising the power to acquire land (whether under s 8[17] or otherwise);
–   when a trustee is exercising any other powers in relation to land;
–   when a trustee enters into arrangements for the appointment of agents, custodians or nominees[18], or carries out reviewing duties under s 22;
–   when a trustee compounds liabilities under s 15 of the Trustee Act 1925 or any other equivalent power[19];
–   when a trustee insures trust property[20];
–   when dealing with reversionary interests, valuations or audits under s 22(1) or (3) of the Trustee Act 1925, or any equivalent powers[21].

One of the most crucial points to note is that the duty of care is applied to the exercise of powers derived not only from the Act, but also to the exercise of powers 'however conferred'[22]. Trustees of trusts created before commencement of the Act are therefore subject to the duty of care to the same extent as trustees of trusts created after.

Investment

2.11   Paragraph 1(a) of Sch 1 to the Act provides that the statutory duty of care applies to trustees 'when exercising the general power of investment or

---

14   It is, of course, open to a trustee to exclude or limit the scope of the duty, and to lower the standard of care to be expected, by requiring the settlor to insert an exemption clause into the trust deed before accepting an appointment: see paras **2.39** *et seq.*
15   See para **2.11**.
16   See para **2.13**.
17   See para **2.15**.
18   See para **2.19**.
19   See para **2.24**.
20   See para **2.27**.
21   See para **2.28**.
22   Trustee Act 2000, Sch 1.

any other power of investment, however conferred'. In itself, para 1 is relatively straightforward: if a trustee is investing the trust's funds, he owes a duty of care, and accordingly must exercise his powers with 'reasonable care and skill'. However, the drafting of para 1 applies the duty only 'when exercising' the investment powers, and thus a failure to exercise investment powers does not constitute a breach of the statutory duty of care.

2.12 The omission from the scope of the duty of care of the situation where a trustee fails to invest at all (as opposed to investing negligently) does not prejudice the interests of beneficiaries, as the trustee is already under a separate duty to invest the trust fund, and will be called to account for any loss occasioned by his failure to do so[23].

2.13 The duty of care also applies to trustees 'when carrying out a duty to which he is subject under section 4 or 5'[24]. Section 4 requires a trustee to have regard to the 'Standard Investment Criteria' and s 5 requires trustees to take appropriate investment advice[25]. As with para 1(a), the drafting of para 1(b) states that the duty of care applies when trustees carry out their duties, and therefore seemingly does not apply in relation to a failure by them to carry out the duty at all. However, it is submitted that a failure to perform the duties under ss 4 and 5 may well constitute a breach of the duty of care 'when exercising the general power of investment or any other power of investment, however conferred'[26] in that the duties under ss 4 and 5 are an integral part of carrying out the wider investment powers (under s 3) properly.

2.14 Further, in the authors' view, a failure to comply with the duties under s 4 or s 5 renders an investment unauthorised[27], and constitutes a breach of trust by the trustee. Accordingly in such situations, the beneficiaries under the trust will have the right to call the trustee to account, and make good any deficiency in the trust fund by means of an account and/or equitable compensation.

Acquisition of land

2.15 Schedule 1, para 2 applies the statutory duty of care to situations where trustees exercise their powers to acquire land, or their other powers in relation to land which they have acquired.

2.16 Paragraph 2(a) of Sch 1 provides that the duty of care applies when trustees exercise their power to acquire land under s 8 of the Act. The duty of care also applies where trustees use similar powers conferred otherwise, for

---

23   See, for example, *Stafford v Fiddon* (1857) 23 Beav 386.
24   Schedule 1, para 1(a).
25   For a detailed discussion of the provisions of ss 4 and 5, see paras **3.23** *et seq.*
26   See para **2.11**.
27   See para **3.44**.

example by the trust instrument[28]. Again, the Schedule provides that the duty of care will apply only if and when the trustees exercise their powers of acquisition, and not where they fail to do so, as they are stated to be subject to the duty 'when exercising' those powers. However, as trustees are under no positive duty to acquire land[29], it would be wrong for the Act to apply the duty of care to situations where trustees do not exercise their powers. Of course, if it can be shown that a particular investment in land should have been made[30], a failure to purchase may constitute a breach of the duty of care, but in relation to the investment powers.

2.17   The duty also applies where trustees are exercising any powers they have in relation to land acquired by the trustees in exercise of their powers mentioned above[31]. As the duty applies to trustees 'when exercising' the powers in relation to land, the duty does not apply to a failure by them to use those powers. However, unlike the situations where a trustee fails to invest[32] or fails to comply with the duties under s 4 or s 5 of the Act[33], it would seem that a beneficiary aggrieved at a trustee's decision not to use such powers may not be sufficiently protected, as there is no established duty imposed upon the trustee to use the powers per se. It may be argued, in certain circumstances, that a failure to use the powers might constitute some other breach of the trustee's duties (eg a failure to grant a lease over an investment property could be argued to be a failure to invest properly) but the success of such an argument would be by no means certain.

2.18   The omission of any statutory remedy for a beneficiary in circumstances where trustees fail to use their powers in relation to land (other than acquisition) is a serious one. It is less of a problem where the defaulting trustee is a personal representative[34], as a beneficiary would have the possible remedy of bringing a claim for *devastavit*. However, where an *inter vivos* trust is involved, beneficiaries would be forced to resort to a claim under the so-called 'common law' duty of care discussed below[35].

Agents, nominees and custodians

2.19   The statutory duty of care is applied by para 3 of Sch 1 to situations where trustees use their powers to employ agents, custodians and nominees. It applies in the following situations: when trustees enter into arrangements

---

28   Schedule 1, para 2(b).
29   Other than any which may be imposed by the trust instrument, a breach of which will give rise to an action for breach of trust.
30   For example, as a result of advice sought under s 5.
31   By virtue of Sch 1.
32   See para **2.12**.
33   See para **2.13**.
34   To whom the Act applies by virtue of s 35.
35   At para **2.48**.

under which an agent is appointed[36]; when they do so in relation to nominees[37] or custodians[38]; and when a trustee carries out review duties under s 22 of the Act[39]. The duty applies equally to appointments made by trustees using their powers under the Act, or otherwise[40].

2.20 Examples of matters likely to constitute breaches of the statutory duty in relation to appointing agents are: failing to ensure that sufficient 'powers of intervention' are retained when delegating[41]; failing to provide a suitable or adequate investment policy[42]; and appointing an unsuitable agent[43].

2.21 Where a trustee fails to delegate, there will not normally be a breach of the statutory duty of care[44]. However, as with the failure to use powers in relation to land, there may be circumstances in which a beneficiary will be able to show that a failure to delegate constitutes a breach of the duty in some other context. For example, if a trustee fails to delegate to an investment manager (thereby losing the opportunity to take advantage of certain types of investment) that failure to delegate may be actionable as a breach of the duty of care in relation to the trustee's investment duties.

2.22 The position in relation to a failure by the trustee to carry out his review obligations under s 22 is also problematical. As with the instances discussed above, the drafting of the Act suggests that a complete failure to fulfil such obligations does not result in a breach of the duty of care, as the duty applies only to the trustee 'when carrying out' the duties imposed by s 22. This is the situation in which the somewhat loose drafting causes problems for aggrieved beneficiaries, in that there would seem to be no remedy for a failure to carry out the s 22 duties, other than a claim under the common law duty of care, provided the effect of s 23 of the Act is not to exclude all liability for a failure to review by trustees[45].

2.23 If the common-law duty does still apply, the aggrieved beneficiary will be required to bring an action, on the basis that the trustee has failed to

---

36   Schedule 1, para 3(1)(a).
37   Ibid, para 3(1)(b).
38   Ibid, para 3(1)(c).
39   Ibid, para 3(1)(e).
40   Ibid, para 3(1)(d).
41   As referred to in s 22(1)(b). See Sch 1, para 3(2)(b).
42   As required by s 15(2)(a).
43   Schedule 1, para 3(2)(a).
44   By virtue of Sch 1 seemingly applying the statutory duty of care to acts, but not to omissions.
45   See para **5.44**.

administer the trust with reasonable care and skill[46]. Further, as a result of the repeal of ss 23 and 30 of the 1925 Act[47], the standard by which trustees' conduct is to be judged in this context is that which applied before 1926[48].

Compounding of liabilities

2.24   Trustees are also subject to the statutory duty of care when exercising their powers under s 15 of the 1925 Act[49] or any corresponding power, however conferred[50]. The powers given to trustees by s 15 of the 1925 Act are as follows:

–   the power to accept any property (real or personal) before the time at which it is made transferable or payable[51];
–   the power to sever or apportion any blended trust funds or property[52];
–   the power to pay or allow any debt or claim on any evidence that the trustee(s) think sufficient[53];
–   the power to accept any composition or security (real or personal) for any debt or property claimed[54];
–   the power to allow any time for payment of debt[55];
–   the power to compromise, compound, abandon, submit to arbitration, or otherwise settle any debt, account, claim or thing whatever relating to the estate (whether testate or intestate) or trust[56].

2.25   The application of the statutory duty of care to these powers has necessitated amendment of the relatively wide exemption contained within s 15 of the 1925 Act. Prior to amendment[57], s 15 contained an exemption from liability in terms that a trustee is not responsible '. . . for any loss occasioned by any act or thing so done by him in good faith'. The Act has replaced the words 'in good faith' with 'if he has or they have discharged the duty of care set out in section 1(1) of the Trustee Act 2000'. The impact on trustees should not be underestimated: whereas prior to the passage of the Act all liability for acts in good faith was excluded, all trustees exercising s 15 or similar powers must now comply with the duty of care, and act with such care as is 'reasonable in the circumstances', a much higher threshold for them to pass.

---

46   See para **2.48**.
47   Schedule 4.
48   See para **2.59**.
49   Schedule 1, para 4(a).
50   Ibid, para 4(b).
51   Trustee Act 1925, s 15(a).
52   Ibid, s 15(b).
53   Ibid, s 15(c).
54   Ibid, s 15(d).
55   Ibid, s 15(e).
56   Ibid, s 15(f).
57   By Sch 2, para 20 to the Trustee Act 2000.

2.26 The reason for applying the duty of care in this context has been stated by the Lord Chancellor as the need for consistency[58]. With the repeal of s 23 of the 1925 Act, the standard of 'good faith' has been removed from perhaps its most important place in the 1925 Act. The decision therefore appears to have been taken to remove it entirely from the 1925 Act and replace it with the statutory duty of care. Any approach which increases consistency within legislation should be welcomed. However, what must not be overlooked is the fact that the change results in a duty of much wider scope being owed by trustees to beneficiaries. This is so notwithstanding the fact that there has been no extension of the s 15 powers by the Act, and therefore no obvious need to increase the safeguards for beneficiaries.

Insurance

2.27 Paragraph 5 of Sch 1 provides that the statutory duty of care applies to trustees when exercising their power under s 19 of the 1925 Act[59] to insure trust property, or any equivalent power howsoever conferred. Again, the anomalous position is created of a trustee being subject to the statutory duty of care if he insures trust properly in a negligent manner (eg failing to insure a particular risk, or failing to pay a policy premium with the result that the policy lapses) but not if he fails to insure the property at all. The law is not entirely clear as to whether trustees are in fact under a positive duty to insure trust property[60], and it would seem that the opportunity provided by the introduction of the duty of care to clarify the position (by expressly imposing such a positive duty) has been missed.

Reversionary interests, valuation and audit

2.28 The statutory duty of care applies to trustees when exercising their power under s 22(1) or (3) of the 1925 Act, or to do any of the things referred to therein[61]. It also applies when exercising similar powers, however conferred[62]. The matters referred to are as follows:

- agreeing or ascertaining the amount or value of property not vested in the trustees or choses in action upon their falling into possession of the trustees[63];
- accepting in or towards satisfaction thereof (at current or market value, or upon any valuation or estimate which they may think fit) any authorised investment[64];

---

58 Hansard, 7 June 2000, at para CWH 13.
59 As amended by s 34 of the Act.
60 See para **7.10**.
61 Schedule 1, para 6(a).
62 Schedule 1, para 6(b).
63 Section 22(1)(a).
64 Section 22(1)(b).

– allowing any deductions for duties, costs, charges and expenses which they think proper or reasonable[65];

– executing any release discharging accountable parties from liability in respect of the matters contained in the release[66];

– ascertaining and fixing the value of any trust property in such manner as they think proper[67].

2.29   As with s 15 of the 1925 Act[68], the test of 'good faith' is replaced by the statutory duty of care, for the sake of consistency throughout the 1925 Act after the abolition of the good faith test in s 23. Again, it should be noted that the imposition of the statutory duty of care has the effect of widening the scope of trustees' duties in this context, and impacts upon all exercises of the powers outlined above, regardless of whether they derive from legislation or the trust instrument. It also applies to trusts pre-dating the Act, as well as new trusts.

Exclusion of omissions from scope of duty of care

2.30   It is tempting to criticise the drafting of Sch 1 to the Act by reason of its failure to extend the statutory duty of care to situations where trustees omit to carry out functions under the Act. However, to do so would be unfair, as the limited scope of the statutory duty appears to be intentional. When introducing the Trustee Bill in the House of Lords, Lord Irvine of Lairg LC made the following comment:

> 'This new duty will apply to the way trustees exercise discretionary power. It will not apply to a decision by the trustees as to whether to exercise that discretionary power in the first place.'[69]

2.31   The question to be answered is therefore: why? The answer, it would seem, relates to insurance. In the Consultation Document, the Law Commission recommended that the Act impose a positive duty to insure trust property, in situations where 'a reasonable prudent person would have insured the property'[70]. However, the responses to the Consultation Paper were largely opposed to the imposition of such a duty for the reasons listed by the Law Commission in its report[71].

---

65   Section 22(1)(c).
66   Section 22(1)(d).
67   Section 22(3).
68   See para **2.24**.
69   Hansard, 14 April 2000, at para 374, per Lord Irvine of Lairg LC.
70   Law Com Consultation Paper No 146, at para 9.21.
71   Law Com No 260, at para 6.8, in which it stated the following: 'Although the nature of the common law duties of trustees is such that they may sometimes be under a duty to insure in any event, the Commission's provisional proposal to codify this aspect of the law was not endorsed on consultation. The underlying concern of those who objected to the proposal appears to have been the risk of uncertainty as to when the duty would arise, and the fact that this might lead trustees to insure when it was unnecessary, thereby wasting trust assets'. The reaction to the concerns expressed on consultation was to withdraw any proposal for there to be a statutory duty to insure trust property.

2.32   The authors consider that the reluctance to apply the statutory duty of care to the question of whether trust property is insured (and indeed other omissions) makes little sense, especially in light of the existence of the common-law duty of care. First, the standard of care proposed by the Law Commission, whilst differing in the ways noted in this chapter[72], is not too different from that required from trustees at common law, namely to act with the care and skill expected by the ordinary prudent man of business[73], and thus would not have represented any radical shift in the law. Secondly, if the statutory duty of care had been applied to omissions by trustees, no *strict* liability would have been imposed upon them: a trustee would only have been liable for breach of duty if it could be shown that he did not act with the care and skill as was 'reasonable in the circumstances'[74]. Instead, the position which has been created is highly unsatisfactory, with acts and omissions by trustees being judged against slightly different standards of care, and with beneficiaries possibly having to seek different remedies for breach[75]. Further, if it was considered that the problem related specifically to insurance, why was the duty of care not extended to failures by trustees to use other powers, such as the powers to review the activities of their agents? It would seem that the reaction to the perceived problems raised on consultation has, in fact, led to a rather clumsy and inconsistent application of the statutory duty of care.

Parties

2.33   The foregoing discussion deals with the issue of the various activities in relation to which a trustee will be subject to the statutory duty of care. The next important issue to address is that of to whom and by whom the duty is owed.

2.34   The statutory duty of care is expressed to apply to 'a trustee'[76] a term which includes personal representatives[77]. No further definition of 'trustee' is provided by the Act. This may not appear to be problematical, as in the usual case the answer will be clear. However, there are certain cases which merit further consideration.

The Law Commission clearly considered that a necessary part of that was to exclude a failure to insure trust property from the scope of the statutory duty of care. This is evidenced by the comments at para 6.9 of the report: 'Although the Law Commission accepts that the circumstances in which trust property is insured should be left to the discretion of the trustees (and to their common law duties), it is considered that, once the trustees have resolved to exercise their powers of insurance, the manner in which they do should be subject to the statutory duty of care . . .'.

72   See paras **2.48** *et seq.*
73   Ibid.
74   Section 1(1).
75   See para **2.66**.
76   Section 1 and Sch 1, paras 1, 2, 3, 4, 5 and 6.
77   Section 35(1).

Bare trustees/nominees

2.35 In the authors' view, a bare trustee or nominee will not have the powers of investment[78] or the other default powers conferred by the Act, save for the power to insure[79]. The question therefore must be asked: are they subject to the statutory duty of care? It is submitted that they are, but only insofar as they are exercising the powers referred to in Sch 1. This is due to the fact that the statutory duty of care is expressed to apply to trustees exercising the powers referred to 'however conferred'. Thus, if a bare trustee is given powers of investment by a trust instrument, he will, it would seem to follow, be subject to the duty. Indeed, it is submitted that any other outcome would be absurd.

Constructive and resulting trustees

2.36 Similar questions arise in relation to constructive and resulting trustees. As regards resulting trustees the position is relatively straightforward, as they will invariably be bare trustees, and therefore subject to the duty of care to the same extent, save that they will not have any powers conferred other than by the Act. Constructive trustees are more problematical. Certain constructive trustees may be treated as 'proper' trustees and have conferred upon them the default powers under the Act. For example, a trustee de son tort. But again, they would seem to be in the same position to a bare trustee.

Settled land

2.37 Trustees of a strict settlement are clearly within the definition of the term 'trustee'. As for the tenant for life, the Act makes specific provision as to the extent to which the powers and duties under the Act applies to him[80]. A tenant for life is given the powers of a trustee only in relation to the appointment and remuneration of agents, custodians and nominees[81] and the insurance of trust property[82]. Logically, the statutory duty of care is applied to him only in relation to the exercise of those powers[83]. It would seem from the wording of the provisions applying the duty[84] that the duty applies only to the exercise of the powers conferred by the Act, and not 'however conferred'. They state that the duty of care provisions apply 'insofar as they relate to the provisions mentioned in paragraphs (a) and

---

78   See para **3.64**.
79   See para **7.7**.
80   Schedule 2, para 17.
81   See para **5.8**.
82   See para **7.8**.
83   Settled Land Act 1925, s 107(1A)(d) inserted by Sch 2, para 17 to the Trustee Act 2000.
84   Ibid.

(c)'. The provisions in (a) and (c) referred to, are the relevant sections of the Act, and therefore powers conferred by the Act alone are subject to the statutory duty.

2.38 The Act makes no reference to whom the statutory duty of care is owed. Plainly, the duty is owed to the beneficiaries under the trust. However, some English settlors now adopt the hitherto offshore practice of appointing a person or committee as 'protector', giving them rights to control some aspects of the trustees' exercise of their powers. It remains to be seen whether such a person has the right to bring a claim for breach of the statutory duty of care, although the authors' view is that they almost certainly will not, unless also a beneficiary. A further complication would be introduced by a settlor purporting to give the protector the right to bring such an action in the trust instrument, however, the authors are of the view that the courts would be quick to hold such a right to be invalid on the basis that the protector has no proprietary rights in the trust fund. The alternative approach would be to permit the protector to bring such an action on the basis that the protector holds such a right as a fiduciary for the beneficiaries, and would be trustee of any amounts recovered for breach[85].

EXCLUSION OF LIABILITY

2.39 Schedule 1, para 7 provides that the statutory duty of care will not apply '. . . if or in so far as it appears from the trust instrument that the duty is not meant to apply'. This means that as far as the drafting of new trusts is concerned, the duty can be excluded by the insertion into the trust deed of a simple clause to that effect[86]. Further, it is submitted that the provisions of Sch 1, para 7 should also enable a settlor to lower the standard of care to be expected of a trustee by including a clause that states that the statutory duty of care will not apply insofar as it requires a standard of care higher than that stated in the clause itself[87].

2.40 As the Act applies the statutory duty of care to trusts already in existence, as opposed to merely trusts created after the passing of the Act, perhaps the more important issue is whether existing exclusion clauses are sufficient to exclude the statutory duty of care. Although exclusion clauses in pre-Act trusts will not expressly exclude the statutory duty of care, some pre-existing clauses will, in the authors' view, be wide enough in scope to exclude the statutory duty. Therefore, existing clauses must be considered in

---

85   As to whether the claimant would, in fact, receive any sums in the way of damages or compensation as opposed to calling the trustee to account: see paras **2.60** *et seq*.
86   See form K at Appendix III.
87   By excluding, for example, the subjective factors in s 1(1)(a). See form L at Appendix III.

light of the Act to determine whether they have the effect of excluding the statutory duty. It is worth considering some of the examples of exclusion clauses commonly found in modern trusts. The first example is the standard clause provided by the Society of Trust and Estate Practitioners (STEP), which provides as follows:

> 'A Trustee (other than a Professional Trustee) shall not be liable for a loss to the Trust Fund unless that loss was caused by his own fraud or negligence.'

2.41   This clause will not, in the authors' view, serve to exclude the statutory duty of care. The clause excludes all liability except for 'fraud or negligence' which, on a strict construction, would exclude liability for breach of the statutory duty of care, as such liability arises not from 'fraud or negligence' but from the breach of that statutory duty. However, if one compares the key elements of the statutory duty of care with those of common-law negligence the two key factors are identical:

(1)   in both there is a duty of care owed by the trustee to the beneficiary; and
(2)   the standard of care required is that of the 'reasonable' man (or trustee).

Accordingly, it is almost inconceivable that the courts would hold that a breach of the statutory duty of care is not caused by the 'negligence' of the trustee, and that liability is excluded by virtue of a clause in the terms set out above, especially as exemption clauses are construed contra proferentem, that is to say against the person who seeks to rely upon them[88].

2.42   An example of a common form of exemption clause which would, in the authors' view, be sufficient to exclude liability under the statutory duty of care is that considered by the Court of Appeal in the case of *Armitage v Nurse*[89] which was in the following terms:

> 'No Trustee shall be liable for any loss or damage which may happen to [the Trust] fund or any part thereof or the income thereof at any time or from any cause whatsoever unless such loss or damage shall be caused by his own actual fraud.'

2.43   It is clear that this clause is drafted in wider terms than the STEP standard provision, and consequently trustees are liable only for losses attributable to their fraud. Where such a clause is contained within the trust deed, liability for a breach of the statutory duty of care will not arise, so long as the breach is not fraudulent[90].

2.44   *Armitage v Nurse* is of importance in another respect: the determination of what is meant by the term 'fraud' in the context of trustee

---

88   See, for example, *Photo Productions v Securicor* [1980] AC 827.
89   [1998] Ch 241.
90   It should be noted that a trustee's liability for fraud may not be excluded.

exemption clauses. Millett LJ (as he then was) held that the term equates to 'dishonesty', and that a trustee acts dishonestly '[I]f he acts in a way which he does not honestly believe is in [the beneficiaries'] interest[91].' Therefore, if a trustee consciously fails to take the requisite care when exercising his powers on the basis that he is protected by virtue of an exemption clause, he will be acting dishonestly, and will lose the clause's protection.

2.45   It should therefore be stressed that even though a trustee may be given prima facie exoneration from liability for breach of the statutory duty of care by a clause contained in the trust deed, if that fact is relied upon as the basis for, say, failing to consider the standard investment criteria under s 4(1) of the Act, the protection provided by the clause will be lost, due to the trustee's conduct being categorised as dishonest (and therefore fraudulent). The principle enunciated by Millett LJ in *Armitage v Nurse* applies equally to exemption clauses existing prior to the introduction of the Act and those created afterwards.

2.46   Even though many existing forms of exclusion clause will be sufficient to exclude liability for breach of the statutory duty of care, it is prudent for the trust draftsman to incorporate a specific reference to the statutory duty of care for the sake of completeness, and the reader is referred to the precedent[92] as an example of a simple clause which clearly and unambiguously excludes the duty in accordance with Sch 1, para 7.

2.47   One final point which should be noted in the context of trustee exclusion clauses is that it is an area of law in which reform is likely in the near future. During the course of the House of Lords' debates on the Act, the Lord Chancellor gave an undertaking to refer the question of reform of the law on trustee exemption clauses to the Law Commission[93]. This undertaking was given in response to the view expressed in debate that the Act missed the opportunity to restrict the use of exemption clauses by trustees. In light of this, it is likely that Sch 1, para 7 will be the first provision of the Act to be reformed in some way, or even possibly repealed.

---

91   [1998] Ch 241.
92   Form K at Appendix III.
93   Hansard, 14 April 2000, at para 394, per Lord Irvine of Lairg LC.

COMPARISON WITH THE 'COMMON LAW'[94] DUTY OF CARE

2.48 As discussed above[95], the statutory duty of care is not of universal application, and is not intended to be. In many of the situations in which the beneficiary considers that a trustee has failed to administer the trust with the care and skill expected of him, the beneficiary will be required to rely upon the pre-existing duty of care at common law. Interestingly, the Law Commission considers that the new statutory duty of care '... probably represents no more than a codification of the existing common law duty'[96]. In the authors' view, this is incorrect, as there are crucial differences between the common-law and statutory duties of care, some of which can be reconciled and others which cannot.

2.49 It is well established that when investing trust assets, trustees owe a duty of care to beneficiaries[97]. The standard of care expected of them is that set out in *Re Whiteley*[98], namely:

> '... to take such care as an ordinary prudent man would take if he were minded to make an investment for the benefit of other people for whom he felt morally bound to provide.'

2.50 Immediately apparent is the use of different terminology in the Act, which imposes upon trustees a duty to '... exercise such care and skill as is reasonable in the circumstances'[99]. It could be argued that, as a consequence of the different terminology, the basic tests employed by the common law and the Act are different, however, in the authors' view, the two standards can be reconciled relatively simply. Whilst the Act will take account of both objective and subjective standards and adjust the standard of care owed by a particular trustee accordingly[100], it is submitted that there must be a basic, underlying standard of care which is used as a starting point for that exercise of adjustment. That standard is that of the 'reasonable trustee', and will, it is submitted, correspond to that stated by the court in *Re Whiteley*. Of course, the duty of care of only certain lay trustees will be judged by that standard alone, as s 1(1) requires numerous other factors to be taken

---

94   In the authors' view, it is highly doubtful that the use of the term 'common law' (as used by the Law Commission) is appropriate, as the right of the beneficiary to have the trust administered with due care and skill arises in equity, and not under the common law. However, for the sake of simplicity the references herein shall be to the duty of care 'at common law', the term used by the Law Commission.

95   At para **2.10**.

96   Law Com No 260, para 2.35.

97   See *Cowan v Scargill* [1985] Ch 270.

98   (1886) 33 Ch D 347 at 355.

99   Section 1(1).

100 See para **2.3**.

into account. But, in principle, there will be cases in which the standard of care under s 1(1) will be identical to that at common law.

2.51　After starting with the basic standard of care, the Act requires the court to consider the particular expertise to be expected from particular professions and businesses in order to ascertain the precise standard of care owed by a trustee to beneficiaries[101]. In doing so, the statutory duty reflects the common-law position to some extent. That position was declared by the court in *Bartlett v Barclays Bank Trust Co Ltd*[102], in which Brightman J stated:

> 'I am of opinion that a higher duty of care is plainly due from someone like a trust corporation which carries on a specialised business of trust management. A trust corporation holds itself out in its advertising literature as being above ordinary mortals.'

The Act goes further than *Bartlett*, however, in that it not only takes account of the standard to be expected from a particular class of specialist trustees, but also any particular special knowledge or expertise which the particular trustee holds himself out as having[103]. Thus a trust company which holds itself out as being particularly expert, and as being superior to its *competitors* (as opposed merely to lay trustees) will have a higher standard of care imposed upon it under the Act, by virtue of the subjective test applied by s 1(1)(a). At common law, the trustee would merely be judged according to the standard of the reasonable trust company[104]. Accordingly, it is incorrect for the Law Commission to assert that the Act represents a codification of the common-law position[105].

2.52　A further difference between the standard of care under the Act and at common law is the impact of remuneration. At common law, a higher standard of care is owed by a trustee in receipt of remuneration than by one who is not. The principle is as enunciated by Harman J in *Re Waterman's Will Trusts*[106]:

> '... a paid trustee is expected to exercise a higher standard of diligence and knowledge than an unpaid trustee ...'

However, s 1(1) of the Act makes no reference to remuneration as being a relevant factor *in itself* when determining the standard of care owed by a trustee, referring only to 'special knowledge and experience'[107]. It may be that, when considering 'the circumstances' in s 1(1), the court will consider the fact of remuneration, or, alternatively, that it was considered unneces-

---

101　Under s 1(1)(b).
102　[1980] Ch 515 at 534C.
103　Section 1(1)(a).
104　*Bartlett v Barclays Bank Trust Co Ltd* [1980] Ch 515.
105　See para **2.48**.
106　[1952] 2 All ER 1054.
107　See para **2.4**.

sary to differentiate on the basis of remuneration due to the introduction of a right to 'reasonable remuneration' for professional trustees[108] who by virtue of their professional position will owe a higher standard of care by virtue of s 1(1)(b). If the latter is correct, there may well be trusts where 'non-professional' trustees are still entitled to remuneration (to compensate them for their time, for example) and in such cases the trustee may owe a higher duty at common law than under the Act.

2.53   The Act has therefore created a somewhat confused position in that similar and closely related acts and omissions by trustees may give rise to not only fundamentally different claims[109], but those claims would also be judged by different standards when they might both be described as arising from the trustee's single act of negligence, or want of care and skill. Thus the Law Commission's ambition of creating a 'uniform duty of care'[110] remains, in the authors' view, largely unfulfilled.

2.54   One final point in relation to the common-law duty of care, is that nowhere in the Act is an attempt made to repeal or alter it in any way. Thus, there remains the question of whether the new statutory duty replaces the common law duty where it applies, or whether a trustee owes concurrent duties under the statute and at common law. Certainly, the Law Commission's stated intention was that the statutory duty of care is not intended to 'detract in any way from the fundamental common law duties[111].' Thus it may remain possible for an aggrieved beneficiary to bring two claims against a trustee arising out of one single act of default, or at least to bring the two claims in the alternative.

COMPARISON WITH THE TRUSTEE ACT 1925, SECTIONS 23(1), (3) AND 30

2.55   Prior to the introduction of the Act, the liability of trustees in relation to the appointment of agents was governed by ss 23(1), (3) and 30 of the 1925 Act. These provisions have now been repealed[112].

2.56   A trustee's liability in respect of the use of agents, custodians and nominees is governed by the statutory duty of care insofar as the duty is applied in this context by Sch 1[113]. In addition, s 23(1) of the new Act provides for the limitation of liability of trustees for the acts or defaults of their agent, custodian or nominee, by stating that a trustee:

---

108   See Chapter 6 below.
109   See para **2.66**.
110   Law Com No 260, para 3.9.
111   Ibid, para 3.11.
112   Trustee Act 2000, Sch 2, paras 23 and 24.
113   See para **2.19**.

'. . . is not liable for any act or default of the agent nominee or custodian unless he has failed to comply with the duty of care applicable to him, under paragraph 3 of Schedule 1 . . .'

The instances in which a trustee is subject to the duty of care are: (a) when entering into the arrangements for appointment[114]; and (b) when carrying out the duties under s 22 of the Act[115].

2.57   Section 23 appears to create something of an anomaly. By providing that the trustee is not liable for any act or default if the duty of care is complied with in the particular instances in which it applies, it would seem to exclude liability for any default arising from a failure to do something not covered by the statutory duty. For example, the statutory duty applies in respect of the trustees whilst carrying out a review of the activities of his agent, custodian or nominee. It would seem from the language of Sch 1, para 3(1)(e), however, that a failure to carry out any review at all is not subject to the statutory duty at all. Section 23(1) is worded in such a way as to suggest that provided the statutory duty of care is complied with where it applies, the trustee will be excused from all liability for defaults of his agent, custodian or nominee. It would therefore appear that if a trustee fails to carry out any review of the activities of the agent etc, but has complied with the duty of care where required (ie when appointing and reviewing), he will not be liable for any loss caused to the trust. It is, however, extremely unlikely that this was Parliament's intention, and therefore probable that the courts will adopt the approach that the failure to review is a breach of the trustee's duty under s 22, and that s 23 will not protect him in respect of loss arising from it, as it is *his* default, not that of an agent, custodian or nominee.

2.58   The position is, however, far from clear and will have to be resolved by litigation. As stated, the authors consider that s 23 will not be construed so as to confer the wide exemption from liability which it would appear to be capable of conferring. However, the alternative view is far from unarguable, and it can be expected that it will be raised by trustees accused of, for example, failing to carry out their review duties under s 22. There cannot be any doubt that if the latter view is correct, the Act has created an extremely serious lacuna, one which leaves beneficiaries in a somewhat vulnerable position, and less well protected than under the 1925 Act.

2.59   If s 23(1) is construed in the way the authors envisage, a trustee is liable for a failure to review the activities of his agent, custodian or nominee. As the statutory duty of care does not extend to such a default, the trustee is subject to the 'common law' duty of care, as the statutory standards of care contained in ss 23 and 30 of the 1925 Act have been repealed[116]. This means

---

114   Schedule 1, para 3(1)(a), (b), (c) and (d).
115   Ibid, para 3(1)(e).
116   Trustee Act 2000, Sch 2, paras 23 and 24.

that the law has returned to the position as it was pre-1 January 1926, namely that trustees will be judged by the standard of the ordinary prudent man of business[117]. A full discussion of the nature, and extent of that duty is outside the scope of this book, but readers are referred to Part IV of the Law Commission Consultation Document[118] for an impressive summary of the relevant law both pre- and post-1926.

CLAIMS FOR BREACH OF THE STATUTORY DUTY OF CARE

2.60   If a trustee is in breach of the duty of care owed under the Act, the most important questions for an aggrieved beneficiary are, how does one bring a claim in respect of that breach, and what is the remedy for the breach? Unfortunately, the Act gives no clear answer to either of those questions.

2.61   The first difficulty is ascertaining the precise nature of the cause of action which accrues upon breach of the statutory duty of care by a trustee. The Act does not specify the cause of action or remedy available to an aggrieved beneficiary.

2.62   The Act does not say what it intends to do as regards the duty of care. Does it:

(1)   merely reform the common law test?
(2)   impose a wholly new statutory duty of care actionable as such in tort? or
(3)   incorporate a new equitable duty of care as part of the 'trust duties' giving rise to an action in equity?

2.63   The first proposition can be rejected swiftly. The Act does not seek to reformulate or reform the common law standard of care in the circumstances set out in Sch 1. The simple reason is that the Act simply does not say this. It refers to there being a 'duty under subsection (1)'[119] and makes no reference to any alteration to any pre-existing duties in equity or at common law. Whilst the Lord Chancellor may have stated that 'This aspect of the Bill codifies the present position at common law where there is already a duty of care ...'[120], there is nothing to suggest that Parliament has intended merely to reformulate the pre-existing duty, imposing a slightly different standard of care.

2.64   The Act has therefore created a new duty, but what is the nature of that duty? The answer is uncertain, but has important consequences. If the

---

117   *Speight v Gaunt* (1883) 9 App Cas 1.
118   Law Com No 146.
119   Section 1(2).
120   Hansard, 14 April 2000, at para 374, per Lord Irvine of Lairg LC.

Act creates an independent statutory duty, it would seem to follow that any breach would be actionable in tort as a breach of statutory duty. In order for such a breach to be actionable in tort it must be shown that:

(1) the statutory duty in question was intended to give rise to a private law right[121]; and

(2) the breach gives rise to the kind of damage generally remediable in tort.

The first of these requirements is clearly satisfied by the statutory duty of care: it is a private law duty imposed upon trustees. The Act does not seek to impose any form of criminal sanction for non-compliance with the duty, nor does it impose a regulatory structure, both of which would be factors indicating the absence of any private law right. It is more difficult to determine whether the type of damage sustained by a beneficiary would be of a kind 'generally remediable in tort'. Invariably, the loss complained of by a beneficiary will be pure economic loss. The rules in tort are extremely strict, and therefore make the recovery of such loss difficult save in certain specified situations, such as the reliance upon negligent misstatements[122]. Tort has not hitherto had to deal with the question of whether pure economic loss caused by a trustee's want of care and skill is recoverable, as the breach of duty complained of has been an equitable one, and therefore actionable as such. This may, however, be a distinction which the courts may not adopt, choosing to draw a close analogy between actions for the breach of a trustee's duty of care and skill with claims for professional negligence. This is certainly the approach adopted by Neuberger J in the recent case of *Wight v Olswang (No 2)*[123], a case involving alleged breaches of a trustee's equitable duty of care[124], but which was subsequently overturned on appeal.

2.65 More convincing is the proposition that the Act has created a new duty which subsists in equity, as part of the trust itself. Accordingly, a breach will be actionable in equity, with a trustee being required to restore the trust fund if it is shown that he is guilty of a breach of the duty of care, causing a loss to the trust. If this view is correct, an action for breach of the statutory duty of care will take a very similar form to actions brought for breach of a trustee's 'common law' duty of care and skill.

---

121 See *X v Bedfordshire County Council* [1995] 3 All ER 353 at 364, per Lord Browne-Wilkinson.

122 See *Hedley Byrne v Heller & Partners* [1964] AC 465.

123 [2000] WTLR 783.

124 For a more detailed analysis of this decision, see the article by Penelope Reed in *Trusts and Estates Law Journal*, October 2000. The authors' view on this question is that the damage suffered as a result of a breach of the statutory duty of care is not something properly remediable in tort.

2.66   The question of whether an action for a breach of the statutory duty of care lies in tort or equity may seem somewhat academic. However, there are some very real practical difficulties which would arise if the duty were to be actionable in tort. The most obvious problem relates to a beneficiary under a discretionary trust. If such a beneficiary wishes to pursue an action for breach of the statutory duty of care, and seeks damages in tort it will be practically impossible for the beneficiary to quantify (and therefore plead) *his* (as opposed to the trust fund's) loss. This is because under such a trust the beneficiary might never receive any payment. The trustees might decide, quite properly, that the beneficiary in question is not one in whose favour they wish to exercise their discretion. Accordingly, how can such a beneficiary claim to be entitled to damages? In equity, of course, the appropriate remedy is to compel the trustees to reconstitute the trust fund[125], however it is difficult to see how such a remedy can be obtained at common law. A similar problem relates to a situation in relation to a trust under which income is to be accumulated for, say, 20 years. If a breach of the statutory duty of care gives rise to a claim in tort, an aggrieved beneficiary will acquire an immediate right to recover damages from the trustee. Therefore, if the trustee defaults, the beneficiary would be entitled to a payment in respect of his loss before the end of the accumulation period, whereas if the trustee had not been in default, the beneficiary would have had to wait until the end of that period[126].

2.67   The problems highlighted above, and others[127], show that the new statutory duty of care has not introduced the clarity and consistency it was widely hoped it would. The uncertainty as to the nature of the cause of action accruing to a beneficiary in the event of a breach by a trustee is a serious flaw, and one which would not have required a great deal of skill to have avoided. In particular, it will cause great difficulties for litigators who will be required to draft proceedings without knowing the nature of the claim or the remedies available[128]. It must be hoped that the opportunity to resolve the issue will arise soon after the Act has been brought into force, and that the courts decide that the cause of action is equitable as opposed to tortious

---

125   See *Target Holdings v Redferns* [1994] 2 All ER 337 at 348–9, per Peter Gibson LJ.

126   Unless, of course, he could have taken advantage of the rule in *Saunders v Vautier* (1841) 4 Beav 115 and put an end to the trust.

127   For a convincing argument as to why trustees should not be subject to tortious liability as well as in equity, listing and discussing the potential problems in greater detail, see Nicholas Warren QC: 'Trustee risk and liability' (1999) *Trust Law International* Vol 13, No 4 at pp 230–231.

128   In order to assist in this regard, the authors have prepared precedents of a claim form, particulars of claim, and defence for an action for breach of the statutory duty of care. See forms H and I at Appendix III.

which, in the authors' view, would be the only satisfactory resolution for the reasons given above.

2.68 The Act does not make any reference to the procedure to be employed by a beneficiary when bringing a claim for breach of the duty of care. It must therefore be assumed that procedurally any such claim is to be treated as either an ordinary tortious claim for breach of statutory duty (if it is actionable as such) or as a claim for breach of trust. For details of the relevant practice and procedure, reference should be made to publications dealing in detail with such matters in the context of these types of claim [129].

2.69 The introduction of a statutory duty of care for trustees promised to be a positive development by introducing clarity, certainty and consistency to what was hitherto a complex and sometimes obscure area of law [130]. However, the duty introduced by the Act is open to considerable criticism in that it has given rise to far more questions than it has resolved, as can be seen from the various points raised in this chapter. Whether the statutory duty can be workable in practice, and provide the safeguard it was intended to, remains to be seen. It must therefore be hoped that the courts are able to resolve the ambiguities and other problems which the Act creates, thereby enabling the duty of care to be a more effective remedy than the common law duty which it purports to improve upon.

REVIEWING EXISTING TRUSTS

2.70 Perhaps the biggest impact of the statutory duty of care in practical terms, is that trustees will (as a matter of best practice) have to re-appraise the administration of their trusts in light of it, considering whether the various policies in place are 'reasonable' according to the new objective/ subjective standard by which they are now to be judged. As the duty applies to both pre- and post-Act trusts and also where the trustees are exercising powers under the trust instrument and not the Act, this exercise will have to be carried out in respect of almost every trust. In order to minimise the scope for attack by beneficiaries, the initial review should be carried out as soon as possible, with others regularly thereafter. Unfortunately, the various ambiguities highlighted above will make it difficult for a trustee to determine with complete confidence whether they are fulfilling their duty of care or not. However, the fact that the trustees have reviewed the operation of the trust

---

129 For the practice and procedure relating to claims for breach of trust, the reader is referred to *Chancery Practice and Procedure* (Jordans, 2001), ch 11.
130 In particular, the meaning of s 23 of the Trustee Act 1925 as discussed in *Re Vickery* was particularly worthy of criticism.

on a regular basis will almost certainly be of assistance to the trustees in defending a claim for breach of the duty of care.

2.71 Whilst the various aspects which must be considered by trustees will vary from trust to trust, set out below are some of the factors which it is suggested ought to be considered by trustees when carrying out a review of their trusts. The list is far from exhaustive, and not all questions will be appropriate for each trust.

(1) Investments
  –   To what extent are the new 'standard investment criteria' being fulfilled?
  –   How regularly is the investment portfolio reviewed?
  –   Should there be more regular reviews of the portfolio?
  –   What arrangements are in place for taking proper advice in relation to investments?

(2) Acquisition of land
  –   Is any land being held by the trust being put to the use providing the maximum return possible?
  –   If not, is there a good reason for it not being?

(3) Delegation
  –   Should any of the trustee's functions be delegated to an agent, custodian or nominee?
  –   If any delegation is to take place, are the terms as favourable to the trust as they could be?
  –   If they are not, is there a good reason for this?
  –   Is the policy statement required under s 15 appropriate?
  –   Is there sufficient provision for review of the delegate's activities?

(4) Insurance
  –   Is trust property insured against all the risks which the trustees consider are reasonably likely?
  –   If not, is there a good reason why not? (eg a bare trust where the beneficiaries have directed the trustees not to)

(5) Exemption Clauses
  –   Do existing clauses serve to exclude the statutory duty of care?

2.72 Due to the ambiguities in relation to the meaning and effect of a number of the new provisions, trustees undertaking an initial review of their trusts are unlikely to be open to criticism for seeking advice as to the extent to which their administration of the trusts fulfils the requirements of the duty of care under the Act, provided the expenses incurred are reasonable, and therefore not disproportionate to the size of the trust fund.

SUMMARY

2.73   There follows a summary of the provisions to the statutory duty of care.

(1) Trustees are subject to the statutory duty of care in the circumstances set out in Sch 1 to the Act, and only in those circumstances. The statutory duty of care does not apply to failures to do the things set out in Sch 1 [131].

(2) The statutory duty of care applies to trusts pre-dating the Act.

(3) The standard of care expected from trustees is that which is 'reasonable in the circumstances', taking into account both objective and subjective factors [132].

(4) The so-called 'common law' duty of care has not been abolished by the introduction of the statutory duty of care [133].

(5) The statutory duty of care will not apply if the trust contains a clause to that effect [134].

(6) It is not clear whether a breach of the statutory duty of care gives rise to a claim for breach of statutory duty or of an equitable duty. It is probably the latter [135].

---

131 Paragraph **2.10**.
132 Paragraph **2.3**.
133 Paragraph **2.48**.
134 Paragraphs **2.39** *et seq.*
135 Paragraphs **2.60** *et seq.*

Chapter 3

POWERS OF INVESTMENT

'There are few ways in which a man can be more innocently employed than in getting money.'[1]

INTRODUCTION

3.1 For many practitioners, the provisions of the Trustee Investments Act 1961 ('the 1961 Act') belong back in the hazy past of trust lectures on trustees' administrative powers. The 1961 Act was never, as a matter of principle, easy to grapple with, and in practice the division of trust funds into narrower and wider range funds and the interrelation of investments made under special powers was a challenge for those unfortunate trustees saddled with an instrument to which the 1961 Act applied.

3.2 All modern trusts, almost without exception, contain express investment clauses enabling the trustees to invest in a wide range of investments and, frequently, the provisions will enable the trustees to invest as if they were absolute beneficial owners of the trust property. This, therefore, raises the question as to the need for and application of the new general power of investment which is contained in s 3 of the Act, and further explained in ss 4 to 7.

3.3 The answer is that not all trusts in existence are modern or well drafted. Trusts have longevity, and an investment clause which may have seemed radical 40 years ago, no longer serves the purpose of trustees attempting to secure capital growth and income for the fund in today's investment market. Furthermore, trusts do sometimes arise under home-made wills (and sometimes, quite inexplicably, wills drafted by professionals) where there is no express investment clause. There are also charitable trusts which have been in existence for a long time, which may have very restrictive investment clauses. Finally, it should not be forgotten that the statutory trusts which arise on intestacy where there are minor beneficiaries rely on a statutory power of investment. All these trusts will be affected by the new provisions.

3.4 Furthermore, the new Act may have ramifications for the trusts draftsman, who may consider, particularly in simple drafts, that it is unnecessary to have an express investment clause in the light of the new provisions[2].

---

1   Dr Johnson to Mr William Strahan, *Boswell's Life of Johnson.*
2   A suggested clause for inclusion of the statutory power is contained as form A in Appendix III.

3.5   Finally, some of the provisions of ss 3 to 7 of the Act apply to the exercise of all powers of investment and not just the general power of investment contained in the Act. Therefore, all trustees have to be familiar with these provisions, even if their trust enjoys an express power of investment which ousts the Act.

3.6   It will be useful, before turning to the new provisions to look, albeit in the briefest possible way, at the terms of the 1961 Act, which when it was passed, revolutionised investment powers for trustees.

SUMMARY OF THE LAW UNDER THE 1961 ACT

3.7   The Trustee Investments Act 1961 defined for trustees the categories of assets in which trust funds could be invested. The aim was to ensure that trustees invested only in safe investments, and to a modern eye the classes of investment set out in Sch 1 to the 1961 Act seem very restrictive.

3.8   In essence, the 1961 Act provided that the fund or any part of it could be invested in the narrower range investments set out in Parts I and II of Sch 1 to the Act. Part I contained investments which could be made without advice [3], and Part II contained investments which could only be made once proper advice has been taken [4]. Part II of the Schedule contained wider range investments, essentially equities fulfilling certain conditions [5]. In order to be able to invest in those, the trustees had to divide the fund so that only one half [6] was invested in wider range investments.

3.9   There were further complications if the trust instrument contained a special power, that is an express power of investment, even if that was only a power to invest in such investment authorised by law from time to time [7]. In such a case, the trust fund had to be divided into three parts, with special range investments, wider range investments and narrower range investments.

3.10   The 1961 Act contained further provisions for maintaining the divisions in the trust fund which affected the funds to which property accruing to the fund should be accredited, as well as the manner in which the funds should be drawn out [8]. All in all, although it contained some useful

---

3   Essentially gilts.
4   Government and local authority bonds and the like and loans on land.
5   These conditions were sufficiently narrow that new issues of shares in public utilities did not fulfil the criteria and Acts dealing with privatisation often dealt with this point so that the new issue was regarded as an authorised investment under the 1961 Act.
6   This was later changed so that 75 per cent of the fund could be invested in wider range securities, see: Trustee Investments (Division of Trust Fund) Order 1996.
7   See s 3(1) of and Sch 2, para 1 to the 1961 Act.
8   See s 2 of the 1961 Act.

concepts (which have been retained at least in part by the new Act) the 1961 Act did not provide the trustees with sufficiently wide powers in the context of the modern world of investments, and made the life of trustees wishing to invest in wider range investments unduly cumbersome. However, by the time of its repeal, amendments had been made to the 1961 Act to enable 75 per cent of the fund to be invested in wider range investments which was not unreasonable and the list of wider range investments had been enlarged to include, for example, stocks and shares issued by the governments of certain European States[9]. From a practical point of view, therefore, the 1961 Act was not quite so outmoded or restrictive in its last years as might elsewhere be suggested.

THE GENERAL POWER OF INVESTMENT

3.11   Section 3(1) of the Act provides trustees with a new wide statutory power of investment so that:

> 'Subject to the provisions of this Part, a trustee may make any kind of investment that he could make if he were absolutely entitled to the assets of the trust.'

Section 3(2) of the Act defines this as 'the general power of investment'.

3.12   The power is clearly a very wide one, and mirrors in simple terms the sort of investment clauses commonly found in modern trusts. In fact, the Law Commission's drafting follows the wording used in s 34(1) of the Pensions Act 1995 which provides a power of investment for the trustees of occupational pension schemes[10]. However, the most commonly found investment clause in modern trusts refers to the trustee being able to invest as if 'absolutely beneficially entitled to the trust assets'. The wording of s 3(1) is somewhat different in that the identity of the trustee is important. He can only make such investments as he could if the assets belonged to him. This will in practice make little difference except perhaps in the case of a corporate trustee with restricted powers of dealing with its own assets.

3.13   The main exception to this wide power is that the power to invest in land[11] other than loans secured on land[12] is excluded[13]. This exclusion is in fact (at least to an extent) illusory, as the power to invest in freehold or leasehold land is contained in s 8 and is dealt with in the following chapter.

---

9   Trustee Investments (Additional Powers) Order (No 2) 1994.
10   Parts II and III of the Act relating to investment and acquisition of land do not apply to the trustees of an occupational pension scheme, see: s 36(3) of the Act.
11   Which term is not defined in the Act, but is defined in the Interpretation Act 1978 and see para **4.15**.
12   See para **3.19** for the definition of this.
13   Section 3(3).

3.14 There is no requirement, as there was under the 1961 Act, for there to be any division of the trust fund, but the power to invest is subject to the safeguards imposed by ss 4 and 5 of the Act which are dealt with below.

THE MEANING OF 'INVESTMENT'

3.15 The Act does not contain any definition of the term 'investment' which in many ways is to be regretted. Traditionally the term 'invest' as used in an investment clause has been construed with an emphasis on the income-producing nature of the asset concerned. In *Re Wragg*[14], Lawrence J defined the word 'invest' in an investment clause in a will as having as one of its meanings:

> 'to apply money in the purchase of some property from which profit or interest is expected and which property is purchased in order to be held for the sake of the income which it will yield.' [15]

3.16 In that case, a wide investment clause authorised the purchase of real estate as an investment. This construction of the word 'invest' if imported into the new general power to invest would restrict the trustees so that non-income producing assets could not be purchased with the trust funds, thereby excluding, for example, works of art, non-income producing bonds and policies, commodities and financial futures. This is why many modern investment clauses after giving the trustees the power to invest as if they were absolute owners, go on to say that the power will apply, whether the asset 'is income producing or not'.

3.17 The emphasis on the property in which in the trust fund is invested producing income is probably not justified in a modern context and in *Harries v Church Commissioners*[16] the Vice-Chancellor, Sir Donald Nicholls said[17] that investment involved the trustees 'seeking to obtain the maximum return by way of income or capital growth which is consistent with commercial prudence'.

3.18 It seems unlikely that a court faced with a trustee who had exercised the general power of investment to purchase antique silver would construe the word 'invest' narrowly, and hold that the purchase was not an authorised investment under the Act, and similarly with any other purchase where capital growth was the objective rather than the production of income,

---

14   [1919] 2 Ch 58.
15   Ibid, at 64–65.
16   [1992] 1 WLR 1241.
17   Ibid, at 1246.

provided of course that in all other respects the trustees had complied with their statutory duty of care[18].

LOANS SECURED ON LAND

3.19   Loans secured on land were permitted as a form of investment even under the provisions of the Trustee Act 1925 ('the 1925 Act')[19], and formed one of the narrower range of investments which required advice under the 1961 Act[20].

3.20   Section 3(4) of the Act defines loans secured on land in a sufficiently wide manner that it would appear to encompass any sort of mortgage or charge, whether legal or equitable. Further, the word 'loan' is widely defined as including where one person provides another with credit[21], and credit includes any cash loan or other financial accommodation[22] and cash includes money in any form[23]. This would clearly cover the case where trustees provided funds for, say, a development project, where any monies advanced were secured by a charge over the land. It is less clear whether financial accommodation is wide enough to cover a guarantee provided by the trustees to secure a primary liability of the mortgagor, charged on land owned by him, but it seems likely that it would. Having said that, such use of trust funds by the trustees is unlikely to be a satisfactory investment.

3.21   The Standard Investment Criteria[24] and the need to consider proper advice[25] and the duty to review investments apply to loans made on land as they do to all other investments, but there are certain specific matters which relate to such investments. For example, trustees will not only need to take advice on whether the loan of trust assets on mortgage would be a suitable investment for the trust in question, but will need to be specifically concerned with the value of the property on which the loan is to be secured and its sufficiency as security for that loan as well as the title to the property. The Trustee Act 2000 repeals s 8 of the Trustee Act 1925 in respect of loans made after the commencement of the new Act[26]. That section provided that a trustee would not be in breach of trust in respect of trust monies loaned on

---

18   As to which, see Chapter 2 above.
19   Section 6, although subject to fairly stringent restrictions.
20   Part II of Sch 1 to the 1961 Act.
21   Section 3(4)(a).
22   Section 3(5).
23   Section 3(6).
24   See para **3.23**.
25   See para **3.32**.
26   Paragraph 2 of Sch 3 to the Act.

mortgage if he had complied with certain conditions[27]. Whilst this section will not apply to loans on land made after the coming into force of the new Act, much of the guidance on advice contained in the section will still be worth heeding. Therefore, a competent surveyor or valuer should be used, he should be independent of the owner of the land and his advice should be sought as to how much can be safely advanced on the security of the property.

3.22 The Trustee Act 2000 also repeals s 9 of the Trustee Act 1925[28] which will, however, continue to apply in respect of loans made on land prior to the coming into force of the new Act[29]. This section provided relief for trustees who lent on mortgage but advanced more than they should have done, but where in all other respects the advance was a proper exercise of their powers of investment. In such a case, they were liable only for the excess they had advanced. This relief will no longer be available in respect of loans on land made after the coming into force of the Act.

THE STANDARD INVESTMENT CRITERIA

3.23 The Standard Investment Criteria provide the safeguards in respect of the wide powers of investment vested in trustees under s 3(1) of the Act. The concepts are not new. They are borrowed from the 1961 Act[30] with some minor redrafting to bring them up to date. It is important to note that s 4(1) provides that trustees must have regard to the Standard Investment Criteria when exercising *any* power of investment whether arising under the Act or otherwise. Therefore, the criteria will apply not only where the trustees have a general power of investment but also where there is an express investment clause in the trust.

3.24 What is more, while the general power of investment is subject to any restriction or exclusion imposed by the trust instrument[31], the duties imposed on trustees by the standard investment criteria cannot be subject to a contrary intention in the instrument creating the trust. In general terms, this was in fact the position under the 1961 Act.

---

27   Essentially, that in making the loan he was acting upon the report of a person whom
     he reasonably believed to be an able practical surveyor or valuer instructed and
     employed independently of the owner, that the amount of the loan did not exceed
     two-thirds of the value of the property and the loan was made under the advice of the
     surveyor or valuer who made the report. In respect of loans on land made before the
     coming into force of the Act, s 8 will still be of importance.
28   Section 40 and Sch 2, para 1(3)(a).
29   Paragraph 3 of Sch 3 to the Act.
30   Section 6(1) of the 1961 Act.
31   Section 6(1)(b) of the Act.

3.25 Trustees must take into account the Standard Investment Criteria when exercising any investment powers, and furthermore they must from time to time review the investments of the trust and consider whether in the light of the Standard Investment Criteria the investments should be varied[32].

3.26 The standard investment criteria are as follows:

– the suitability to the trust of the type of investment of the same kind as any particular investment proposed to be made or retained and of that particular investment as an investment of that kind[33]; and
– the need for diversification of investments of the trust, insofar as is appropriate to the circumstances of the trust[34].

These will be dealt with in turn.

Suitability

3.27 These criteria demand that the trustees look first of all at the type of investment they propose to make (eg in equities, gilts, unit trusts, works of art) to judge whether that type of investment will be appropriate for the particular trust in question, and then to look at the particular investment being considered to see whether it is suitable. So, for example, let us assume that the trustees are proposing to invest the trust fund in unit trusts. The first question which they have to ask themselves is: is a unit trust a suitable investment for this particular trust fund? If the answer to that question is 'yes', they must go on to consider whether the particular unit trust they had in mind will be suitable for their trust and at this stage considerations as to performance of the unit trust, for example, will come into play.

3.28 Questions of suitability of investment for a particular trust will obviously vary from trust to trust. However, factors which might be taken into account when looking at issues of suitability are, for example, investment by pension fund trustees[35] in an investment of such a long-term nature that the trustees would be unable to realise it easily to provide benefits for its beneficiaries. In the case of a small trust fund, an investment in equities of a speculative nature would be unlikely to be suitable.

3.29 It may also be that when adopting the criteria relating to suitability, considerations of a moral or ethical nature will come into play. Can trustees refuse to invest in certain assets because of a moral or ethical objection, for example, to the tobacco industry? In *Cowan v Scargill*[36], Sir Robert Megarry

---

32   Section 4(2).
33   Section 4(3)(a).
34   Section 4(3)(b).
35   Not covered by s 34 of the Pensions Act 1995.
36   [1985] Ch 270.

V-C held that when the purpose of the trust is to provide financial benefits for the beneficiaries (as is usually the case), the best interests of the beneficiaries when the power of investment is being exercised are their financial interests. Moral and ethical considerations cannot come into play unless there is no financial difference between morally or ethically objectionable investments and others. It has been recognised that in a charitable trust, there may be more scope for ethical and moral consider-ations to be taken into account [37]. This is on the basis that, unlike a pension trust, a charitable trust will not have as its main purpose the production of financial benefits. Therefore, for trustees of a cancer research charity to invest in tobacco shares, even if they did represent the best financial return, would be contrary to the whole purpose of the trust. The position is soon to be changed for occupational pension fund trustees [38]. There is, however, no such requirement under the new Act, and a settlor or testator who is anxious for such considerations to play a major part in any investment policy would be wise to spell that out in a wide investment clause in the trust instrument itself [39].

Diversification

3.30   Section 4(3)(b) in effect re-enacts s 6(1)(a) of the Trustee Invest-ments Act 1961. The need for diversification of investments is very much in accordance with the modern portfolio theory of investments. In *Nestlé v National Westminster Bank plc (No 2)* [40], Hoffman J (as he then was) referred to the modern portfolio theory in the following way:

> 'Modern trustees acting within their investment powers are entitled to be judged by the standards of current portfolio theory which emphasises the risk level of the entire portfolio rather than the risk attaching to each investment taken in isolation.' [41]

Therefore, trustees have to ensure that there is a good spread of investments and hence risk.

3.31   The duty to diversify investments applies to the exercise of *all* powers of investment and not just the general power of investment. What is more, it

---

37   *Harries v Church Commissioners* [1992] 1 WLR 1241.
38   By the Occupational Pension Schemes (Investment and Assignment, Forfeiture, Bankruptcy etc) Amendment Regulations 1999, trustees will be required to include in their Statement of Investment Principles 'the extent (if at all) to which social environmental or ethical considerations are taken into account in the selection, retention and realisation of investments'.
39   An example of a possible clause is contained as form B at Appendix III.
40   [2000] WTLR 795 at first instance, Court of Appeal decision not affecting this point reported in [1993] 1 WLR 1260.
41   Ibid, at 115.

cannot be excluded or restricted [42]. However, the duty applies 'in so far as is appropriate to the circumstances of the trust' [43]. There may be trusts where the fund is so small that diversification is simply not practical. Alternatively, the majority holding in a family company may be the main trust asset, which is not an uncommon state of affairs, particularly in tax planning schemes. Probably, in such a situation, the trustees would be able to persuade the court, in the case of any challenge, that diversification was inappropriate. Similarly, the subject matter of the trust might be a single freehold property, which happens sometimes in a will trust, or where a trust has arisen unexpectedly [44], and in such a case the court would almost certainly infer from the nature of the trust that diversification was not appropriate. In the case of trusts, where it is clear on a long-term basis that it will be inappropriate to diversify investments, this could be made clear in a recital.

ADVICE

3.32 Section 5(1) of the Act provides that before exercising any power of investment, whether the general power of investment or otherwise, the trustee must (unless the exception referred to in s 5(3) applies) obtain and consider proper advice [45] about the way in which, having regard to the standard investment criteria, the power should be exercised.

3.33 Section 5(2) of the Act provides that when reviewing the investments of the trust in accordance with the duty imposed by s 4(2) of the Act, the trustee must also obtain and consider proper advice as to the way in which the investments should be varied. There are notable differences between these provisions and those which obtained under the 1961 Act.

3.34 The first difference is that the duty to seek advice now applies not only to the exercise of the general power of investment, but also to the exercise of an express power of investment contained in a trust instrument. Under the old law, the need to seek proper advice was confined to narrower range investments in Part II of Sch 1 to the 1961 Act, and wider range investments. Advice did not need to be sought by trustees investing in a narrower range investment contained in Part I of the Schedule, nor in exercising an express power of investment contained in the trust instrument, unless the express power contained a specific requirement to that effect. It is certainly very rare to see a trust instrument of modern vintage which imposes any requirement on the trustees to seek advice before exercising their powers.

---

42   See para **3.2.4**.
43   The final words of s 4(3)(b).
44   See, for example, *Binions v Evans* [1972] Ch 359.
45   Defined in s 5(4) and, as to which, see para **3.41**.

3.35   However, the change is not perhaps as radical as it might first seem. At common law it is well established that trustees must seek advice on matters which they do not understand which may include investment[46]. Once again, it does not appear that the trust instrument can relieve the trustees of the need to seek proper advice, but from a practical point of view, in most cases, either the exception will apply[47], or the trustees would be extremely foolish not to seek advice before exercising their powers of investment, and should be keen to do so to avoid being fixed with liability.

3.36   The second difference is that the 1961 Act required the advice to be confirmed in writing[48]. There is no longer such a requirement, which reflects the changes in the investment market, and the standards which apply to professional investment advisers regulated by the Financial Services Act 1986. As a matter of good practice and as protection for the trustees, it would seem sensible for any advice still to be recorded in writing, even if it is contained in a faxed document or electronic mail.

3.37   The third difference is that when advice had to be obtained under the 1961 Act, the requirement was a mandatory one, and the failure to comply with it rendered the investment unauthorised. The requirement under s 5 of the Act is not so stringent. It was recognised in the Law Commission Report that it was difficult to define the circumstances in which the need for advice would arise and the nature of the advice which should be obtained[49]. Clearly, it would put an undue burden on a small fund if the trustees of it had to seek advice every time a small amount of money was invested. Similarly, if the trustee of a fund was an experienced financial adviser, it would be unnecessary to insist that every investment decision required the advice of another, perhaps less experienced adviser.

3.38   The Act resolves the problem by providing an exception to the general rule in s 5(3) which provides that:

> 'a trustee need not obtain such advice if he reasonably concludes that in all the circumstances it is unnecessary or inappropriate to do so.'

Whilst the draftsman of the Act was clearly concerned to ensure flexibility, so that the occasions when advice should be taken were not set down in stone, it is not difficult to foresee some of the arguments which the courts will have to face when applying this provision.

3.39   The first point is that the trustee must 'reasonably conclude' that advice is not necessary or appropriate. The concept of a person coming to a reasonable conclusion on a matter is something with which the law is already

---

46   *Cowan v Scargill* [1985] Ch 270 at 289.
47   As to which, see para **3.38**.
48   Section 6(5) of the 1961 Act.
49   See para 2.32 of the Report.

familiar. For example, in the context of landlord and tenant law, there is a wealth of case-law on the reasonableness of a landlord's consent to an assignment. What is clear from those decisions, and indeed other areas of law where such a concept is applied, is that the question is not whether the court would have come to the same conclusion as the trustee, but whether the conclusion the trustee reached was one which a reasonable trustee in all the circumstances of the case could have reached[50].

3.40 The question of when advice will be unnecessary or inappropriate will have to depend on the particular circumstances of the case. The size of the trust will clearly be important; what is appropriate by way of seeking advice in relation to a fund worth several million pounds, may well be an inappropriately heavy burden on a small fund worth several thousand pounds. The nature and purpose of the trust may also be significant as will the way in which it is currently invested. The type of investment being considered must also play a part, although it is unsafe for trustees to assume that just because they are investing in what were narrower range investments without advice under the 1961 Act, the exception in s 5(3) will apply in the new Act. Such a narrower range investment will not necessarily satisfy the Standard Investment Criteria and it may be necessary to seek advice as to whether that is the case or not. Finally, the exception may apply if the trustees are sufficiently skilled and experienced not to need outside advice when making investments on behalf of the trust. Caution must be exercised by trustees when reaching this conclusion. Today's investment market is probably too complex, and perhaps more importantly, too specialised, for trustees to assume that they have all the requisite knowledge and experience. If in doubt, it is probably wiser for the trustees to seek advice. A challenge by the beneficiaries to the accounts on the basis that the cost of seeking advice should not have been incurred is almost certainly a less expensive and troublesome outcome for a trustee who has sought advice than the alternative of not taking advice when required and being found liable for making an unauthorised investment.

3.41 Proper advice is defined in s 5(4) of the Act as being 'the advice of a person who is reasonably believed by the trustee to be qualified to give it by his ability in and practical experience of financial and other matters relating to the proposed investment'[51]. This provision is lifted from the 1961 Act[52], and is mirrored in the Pensions Act 1995, ss 31(4) and 32(3). There is, perhaps surprisingly, a dearth of authority on the operation of these provisions, which may be, in part, due to the fact that although they appear to give room for argument, in practice they are straightforward. Part of the

---

50 See, for example, *Pimms Ltd v Tallow Chandlers in the City of London* [1964] 2 QB 547 at 564.
51 Section 5(4).
52 Section 6(4) of the 1961 Act.

test of whether a trustee has chosen the right adviser is subjective: did the trustee believe that this particular adviser was qualified to give the advice? The other part of the test is clearly an objective one: was that belief a reasonable one? The question is not whether the court would have concluded that the adviser was qualified to give the advice, but whether it was a belief which a reasonable trustee could have held.

3.42   As with the position under the 1961 Act, the duty of the trustees when making or reviewing investments is to obtain and consider proper advice. They do not have to follow it, and if they do not, the investment will not thereby be rendered unauthorised. Having said that, in most cases, trustees will ignore proper advice at their peril, and unless there is good reason for doing so, will be in breach of the statutory duty of care [53].

CHECKLIST ON THE EXERCISE OF THE GENERAL POWER OF INVESTMENT BY A TRUSTEE

3.43   To summarise the position under the new Act, where the statutory power applies [54], trustees must consider the following matters on making an investment of the trust fund.

–   Is the proposed investment one which the trustees have power to make, looking at the general power of investment, any additional powers contained in the trust instrument and any restrictions and exclusions contained therein?

–   Is the intended application of the trust fund actually an investment, in other words will it generate money for the fund (almost certainly nowadays by way of income production or capital growth)?

–   Is the type of investment proposed a suitable one having regard to the nature of the trust?

–   If the type of investment proposed is a suitable one, is the particular investment which the trustees have in mind a suitable one?

–   Is this a trust where it will be appropriate to diversify investments?

–   If it is such a trust, how will this particular investment fit within that objective?

–   Is it unnecessary or inappropriate to seek advice in relation to the investment?

–   If advice ought to be sought who would be best qualified to give it by reason of his practical experience of financial and other matters relating to the proposed investment?

---

53   As to which see paras **3.50** *et seq.*
54   This is dealt with below in paras **3.56** *et seq.*

A similar checklist applies where a trustee is fulfilling his duty of reviewing the investments of the trust.

EFFECT OF UNAUTHORISED INVESTMENT

3.44 A distinction has to be drawn between a trustee who makes an unauthorised investment, which is a breach of trust and the trustee who, while he makes an authorised investment, is in breach of the statutory duty of care to which he is made subject under s 1 of the Act.

3.45 The trustees are given by the Act the very widest powers of investment, and therefore it might be considered at first sight that no investment will be unauthorised at such. However, the answer is not entirely clear. What is the position if the trustees invest without having regard to the Standard Investment Criteria, or without obtaining and considering proper advice under s 5? Clearly, such a lapse on the part of the trustees would be good evidence to support a claim by the beneficiaries for breach of the trustees' duty of care, but would the investment made without regard to the standard investment criteria or proper advice be unauthorised?

3.46 There may be considerable difficulty in establishing that the trustees have failed to have regard to the Standard Investment Criteria, and it might be considered that those matters go more to the question of breach of the trustees' duty of care (although not the statutory duty of care, perhaps) than to breach of trust. In respect of the failure to obtain proper advice, the question of whether the trustees have complied with this obligation or not may be easier to establish (although there will be some room for the trustees to argue that the exception that they need not obtain advice applied). The better view probably is that the power conferred on the trustee by s 3 of the Act, governs which investments will be authorised and which will not, but only if the conditions contained in ss 4 and 5 are met. As the power is so wide, anything falling within the meaning of an investment would be authorised. However, ss 4 and 5 provide the conditions governing the exercise of the general power of investment and a breach of those provisions will mean that there has been an improper exercise of the power of investment and the investment is unauthorised. Support for this view can be found in para 1 of Sch 1 to the new Act which provides that 'the duty of care applies to a trustee when *carrying out* a duty to which he is subject under section 4 or 5' (our emphasis). Therefore, the duty applies where the trustee is carrying out his duties under ss 4 and 5 to consider the suitability of the investment, the diversification of investments and the seeking of advice. It does not apply the statutory duty of care in circumstances where the trustee has failed to observe the Standard Investment Criteria altogether. There might, however, be a breach of the statutory duty of care in that it applies to a trustee exercising the general power of investment.

3.47   There appear to be no reported decisions in England on the point which could equally have arisen under the 1925 Act[55]. The question may not just be of academic interest. If a breach of trust can be established, the trustee is liable to account to the trust by way of restitutionary compensation for the actual loss suffered by the trust, and this will be the case even if a gain is made by reason of the unauthorised investment, but it is not so substantial a gain as would have been made had there been no breach of trust[56]. The court in such a case will not award damages, but will insist that the trustee accounts strictly to the trust for all that it has lost[57]. This is important, as considerations of remoteness, causation and foreseeability do not arise when the court is considering the trustee's duty to account to the trust fund for loss, which has been occasioned because of his breach of trust[58]. All the court is concerned with is what the trust should have received which it has not because of the unauthorised investment, and what has been dissipated by the trustee in making the investment. Having said that, if breach of the statutory duty of care gives rise to a claim for equitable compensation rather than damages, it will not matter how failure to observe the Standard Investment Criteria is regarded[59].

3.48   It is possible that it will be a great deal easier for the beneficiaries to establish loss if it can be proved that the investment is an unauthorised one, as opposed to establishing that the trustees are in breach of their statutory duty of care. It has also been suggested that if the trustees have invested in authorised investments there is a heavy onus on the beneficiaries to establish that the investment should not in fact have been made[60].

3.49   It would have been relatively simple for the Act to be drafted in such a way that it would have been clear whether or not a failure to comply with ss 4 and 5 would render an investment under s 3 unauthorised, or would merely constitute a breach of the statutory duty of care. The matter may well have to be resolved by litigation.

---

55   But see the Scottish case of *Martin v City of Edinburgh District Council* [1988] SLT 329, where failure to obtain advice was regarded as a breach of trust.

56   *Nestlé v National Westminster Bank plc* [1994] 1 All ER 118.

57   *Nocton v Lord Ashburton* [1914] AC 932 and *Target Holdings v Redferns (No 1)* [1994] 2 All ER 337 at 348–349.

58   But see the comments of Millett LJ as he then was in *Bristol and West Building Society v Mothew* [1999] Ch 1 at 17G–18C where he suggests that common-law rules of causation, remoteness of damage and measure should be applied by analogy to cases of equitable compensation, and para **2.60**.

59   See the authors' views on this problem at paras **2.60** *et seq*.

60   *Shaw v Cates* [1909] Ch 389 at 395.

STATUTORY DUTY OF CARE IN RELATION TO INVESTMENTS[61]

3.50 The statutory duty of care is expressly applied to trustees exercising the general power of investment and in carrying out their duties under ss 4 and 5 of the Act to have regard to the Standard Investment Criteria and to review investments and seek advice[62]. It also applies to the exercise of any power conferred by a trust instrument[63]. It is, therefore, something to which all trustees must have regard, and not just those whose investment powers are governed by the Act. It is unclear whether the introduction of the statutory duty of care represents a change to the law, or simply statutory recognition of the common law position, which has always obtained.

3.51 The first point to note is that a trustee now must exercise 'such care and skill as is reasonable in the circumstances having regard to any special knowledge or experience that he has or holds himself out as having ... and if he acts as trustee in the course of a business or profession, to any special knowledge or experience that it is reasonable to expect of a person acting in the course of that kind of business or profession[64].' The common law has always recognised a higher standard of care being visited on a professional remunerated trustee[65], as well as a trustee who professes special expertise in a particular area[66].

3.52 The new statutory formulation of the duty of care does not, perhaps, go any further than the decided cases in the area of investment, save that it is made clear that a lay trustee who has special knowledge or holds himself out as having special knowledge will be expected to exercise skill and care appropriate to that special knowledge[67]. So, for example, a stockbroker acting as a trustee of a local charity, even though he does so as a volunteer, will be expected to display a higher standard of skill and care in the investment of the trust funds than his fellow volunteer trustee who is a brain surgeon. On the other hand, in ascertaining the level of skill to be expected of him, the fact that he is acting gratuitously may well affect what is 'reasonable in the circumstances'.

3.53 As far as trustees acting in the course of a profession or business are concerned, they will be assumed to have the special knowledge and experience it is reasonable to expect of a person in that kind of profession or

---

61 For a general discussion of this topic, see Chapter 2 above.
62 Paragraph 1 of Sch 1 to the Act.
63 Ibid.
64 Section 1(1).
65 *Speight v Gaunt* (1883) 9 App Cas 1; *National Trustees Co of Australia Ltd v General Finance Co of Australia Ltd* [1905] AC 373; *Re Waterman's Will Trusts* [1951] 2 All ER 1054.
66 *Bartlett v Barclays Bank Trust Co Ltd* [1980] Ch 515.
67 Section 1(1)(a).

business, and in exercising their power of investment they will be subject to the standard of skill and care which follows from that special knowledge and experience[68]. It is not difficult to see that this could prove to be a very difficult test to apply in practice. Is it to be expected that a high street solicitor who perhaps acts as trustee to only one trust, should be subject to the same standard of care which would apply to solicitor who has spent 25 years in the private client department of a leading London firm? Both are solicitors, but their special knowledge and experience are widely different. Arguably, a much higher standard of care should apply to the latter. Notwithstanding this, s 1(1)(b) of the Act appears to envisage that all persons engaged in a particular profession will be expected to have certain special knowledge and experience. It is then for s 1(1)(a) of the Act to raise the standard expected of the private client solicitor who will have to exhibit even greater skill[69]. While these provisions apply to the new statutory duty of care generally, they are of particular importance in relation to the general power of investment where special knowledge and experience on the part of the trustee may be crucial.

3.54 On the assumption that the new Act does not alter the substance of the duty of care owed by a trustee in exercise of the general power of investment, save possibly as set out above, the common law relating to the duty of care owed by a trustee when exercising a power of investment is well developed. The following principles can be derived from the decided cases.

(1) In investing the trust fund, trustees must take such care as an ordinary prudent man would take if he were minded to make an investment for the benefit of other people for whom he felt morally bound to provide[70].

(2) The trustee must avoid all investments even if authorised by the settlement or by statute which are attended with hazard[71].

(3) Trustees, in considering an investment, must consider future and present beneficiaries and hold the scales impartially between them[72]. This means that a trustee should not invest in a high income investment to benefit a life tenant under the trust at the expense of capital growth on behalf of the remainderman[73]. The formulation of this principle was modified by Hoffman J at first instance in *Nestlé v National Westminster*

68   Section 1(1)(b).
69   See the discussion of this at paras **2.5** *et seq.*
70   *Re Whiteley* (1886) 33 Ch D 347 (CA).
71   *Re Whiteley* (1887) 12 App Cas 727 at 733 (HL).
72   *Cowan v Scargill* [1985] Ch 270 at 287.
73   *Re Mulligan deceased* [1998] 1 NZLR 481, which provides a very helpful analysis of the law in this area.

Bank plc[74], where he considered that the duty of the trustees was not to act impartially[75], but to take into account in determining their investment policy the fact that the tenant for life was well known to the settlor, whereas the remainderman may have been a relative stranger. So, for example, in a case where the widow of the settlor was the tenant for life and in straitened circumstances, and the remainderman was a charity, on the basis of Hoffman J's statement of the law, the trustees would be entitled to pursue an investment policy which produced high income yield for the widow, perhaps at the expense of the remainderman. This approach of Hoffman J was approved by the Court of Appeal, at least in substance[76].

(4) A trustee must take advice on matters he does not understand, which principle is now of course enshrined in the new Act. On receiving that advice, his duty is to consider it as a prudent man would and only to reject it if he is acting as a prudent man, and not just because he disagrees with it[77].

(5) A trustee can, in making an investment decision, take into account his own interests, but he must balance these fairly with the interests of the beneficiaries[78].

(6) A trustee must not put himself in a position where his own interests in making investment decisions conflict with his duties to act in the best interests of the beneficiaries[79].

3.55   There is no reason to suspect that the new Act will change these basic principles, save that more attention may have to paid to the status of the trustees, with the mistakes of the inexperienced lay trustee being treated as less culpable than those of the Bank trust company. Having said that, the courts have shown a marked reluctance to fix trustees with liability if they have pursued an unfortunate investment policy, even when those trustees have been leading clearing banks[80]. The important point to note is that trust investments may prove to be a disaster without any lack of care, as such, on the part of the trustees. A mere error of judgement will not necessarily amount to negligence.

---

74   [2000] WTLR 795.
75   See also *Edge v Pensions Ombudsman* [2000] 3 WLR 79 at 100.
76   [1993] 1 WLR 1260 at 1270–1272, 1279.
77   *Cowan v Scargill* [1985] Ch 270 at 289.
78   *X v A* [2000] 1 All ER 490.
79   See *Wight v Olswang* (2000) unreported, 7 December, CA, allowing an appeal against the decision of Neuberger J who had held that unless the investment decisions made were such that no reasonable trustee, looked at objectively, could have made them, the trustee would not be liable.
80   National Westminster Bank plc has escaped liability twice in *Nestlé v National Westminster Bank plc* (above) and *Galmerrow Securities Ltd v National Westminster Bank plc* (1993) unreported, 20 December.

SCOPE OF THE GENERAL POWER OF INVESTMENT AND CONTRARY INTENTION

3.56   The general power of investment is intended to be a default power, in the same way that the powers conferred by the Trustee Investments Act 1961 were intended to be default powers. Consequently, s 6 of the Act provides that the general power of investment is:

> 'in addition to powers conferred on trustees otherwise than by this Act, but subject to any restriction or exclusion imposed by the trust instrument or by any enactment or any provision of subordinate legislation.'[81]

'Subordinate legislation' means Orders in Council, orders rules, regulations, schemes, warrants, byelaws and other instruments made or to be made under any Act, including any local personal or private acts[82].

3.57   Therefore, in the case of a trust instrument which contains an express, wide power of investment, the trustees will have the general power of investment (as indeed they had powers under the 1961 Act) but they will not need to use those powers.

3.58   The general power of investment applies to trusts whether created before or after the commencement of the Act[83]. For trusts created after the commencement of this part of the Act, restricting or excluding the general power of investment will be straightforward[84]. The position is equally clear in respect of trust instruments made before 3 August 1961[85], the date on which the 1961 Act came into force. Section 1(3) of the 1961 Act provided that only instruments made after that date could limit or exclude the powers conferred by the 1961 Act. This was to ensure that restrictive investment clauses in old trusts and wills did not prevent trustees exercising the powers conferred by the Act, which in 1961 were considered to be wide. The whole object of the 1961 Act would have been defeated if the new statutory powers could not be exercised by trustees subject to very restrictive investment powers, who were the very people the Act was designed to assist. The new Act therefore takes care not to re-activate old provisions which might have the effect that trustees of old settlements who have enjoyed powers under the 1961 Act would be prevented from enjoying the new general power of investment because of the restrictions in the old settlement. Therefore, s 7(2) of the new Act provides that:

---

81   Section 6(1)(a) and (b) of the 1961 Act.
82   Section 21.
83   1 February 2001.
84   See form C at Appendix III.
85   The better view is probably that a will is 'made' on the date of its execution, or if confirmed by later codicil, the date of execution of the codicil and not the death of the testator, when the will takes effect.

'No provision relating to the powers of a trustee contained in a trust instrument made before 3 August 1961 is to be treated (for the purposes of section 6(1)(b)) as restricting or excluding the general power of investment.'

3.59 The question of course arises as to when an instrument is 'made' for the purposes of s 7(2). This question is particularly important in respect of wills and appointments made after 3 August 1961 under a special power contained in settlements and wills made before 3 August 1961. In respect of the first question, the better view is probably that a will is 'made' on the date of its execution, or if confirmed by later codicil, the date of execution of the codicil and not the death of the testator, when the will takes effect. As far as the second question is concerned, while appointments for many purposes[86] must be treated as made at the time of the settlement or will, there seems to be a great deal of sense in treating an appointment as made when actually executed. This is on the basis that the appointors were aware after 3 August 1961 of the existence of the Trustee Investments Act 1961, and could therefore choose whether or not to restrict or exclude it.

3.60 The Law Commission did not wish to apply the approach which had been taken in the 1961 Act to the new Act, by rendering restrictions or exclusions in trust instruments made after 3 August 1961 redundant[87]. It considered that restrictions and exclusions included in trust instruments after the coming into force of the 1961 Act should be respected, as to do otherwise would be to ignore the express wishes of the testator or settlor. Therefore, in trust instruments or wills made after the coming into force of the 1961 Act, but before the coming into force of the new Act, restrictions contained in those trusts or wills will have the effect of excluding or restricting the general powers of investment. Examples might be where the settlor has directed that investment should be on a particular ethical basis[88], or where the settlor has had particular reasons for restricting the powers of investment[89]. It will therefore be important to look carefully at the provisions of all trust instruments and wills made after 3 August 1961 to ensure that the investment provisions are not more restrictive than the powers conferred by the new Act.

3.61 What amounts to a restriction or exclusion should not in most cases give rise to any difficulty. A direction in the trust instrument that the trustees may invest in certain assets (eg particular equities) will not without more amount to a restriction as the general power of investment is conferred 'in

---

86   Such as excessive accumulations.

87   See para 2.51 of the Report.

88   Which would not in the absence of a specific direction be possible after *Cowan v Scargill* (above).

89   For example, where the trust was to be for a short duration only.

addition to powers conferred by trustees otherwise than by this Act'[90]. On the other hand, if the trust instrument provides that the trustees can invest in particular equities 'and no other form of investments', that will amount to an express restriction[91]. However, where the provisions of the trust or the will merely confer on the trustees the powers of investment contained in the 1961 Act, or those authorised by law, the new Act treats that power as conferring the general power of investment[92].

3.62   The general power of investment also does not apply to trustees 'who immediately before its commencement have special statutory powers of investment'[93]. A special statutory power of investment is defined as such if it is a power of investment 'conferred by an enactment or subordinate legislation on trustees of a particular trust or particular kind of trust.'[94]. The Act specifically provides that Parts II and III relating to investment and acquisition of land do not apply to occupational pension fund trustees[95], or to the trustees of unit trusts[96] or trustees managing common investment funds or common deposit funds made under the Charities Act 1993[97].

3.63   The Act recognises that it may be desirable to substitute such statutory powers with the new general power of investment and, indeed, a number of the consequential amendments to legislation in Sch 2 to the Act achieve this. As a consequence, the ability to change legislation in the future is preserved[98].

APPLICATION TO BARE TRUSTEES AND IMPLIED TRUSTEES

3.64   It is unfortunate that there is no exhaustive definition of 'trustee' in the new Act. What is more, on the strict wording of s 3 the general power of investment applies to 'a trustee'. The first question is whether this would include a bare trustee or nominee. Strictly, it seems that it would, and the provisions in relation to the new power to insure[99] certainly envisage those powers applying to a bare trustee. There is, however, something odd in the

---

90   Section 6(1)(a) of the 1961 Act, and see *Re Burke* [1908] 2 Ch 248, a case on the Trustee Act 1893.

91   *Ovey v Ovey* [1900] 2 Ch 524.

92   Section 7(3). It seems that even without this provision in the Act, the general power of investment as it is in addition to all other powers conferred would apply.

93   Section 7(1).

94   Section 7(3).

95   Section 36(3). They do of course have identical powers under s 34 of the Pensions Act 1995.

96   Section 37. Section 81 of the Financial Services Act 1986 gives the Secretary of State power to make regulations regarding the investment of such funds.

97   Section 38, and see ss 24 and 25 of the Charities Act 1993.

98   Section 41.

99   As to which, see Chapter 7 below.

concept of a bare trustee having the full panoply of investment powers conferred by the Act when his sole function is to act under the direction of the beneficial owner. If the provision is tested, it is the authors' view that a court would hold that a bare trustee does not have the general power of investment.

3.65 Similar concerns apply in respect of constructive and resulting trustees. Sometimes such trustees are trustees in a true sense [100] but, in many cases, it will clearly be highly inappropriate for such trustees to have the general power of investment. The reference throughout the Act to the trust instrument does seem to render it most unlikely that implied trustees are intended to be covered by the Act.

SUMMARY

3.66 There follows a summary of the provisions in relation to investment.

(1) There is now conferred on trustees a general power of investment which enables them to make any kind of investment that they could make if they were absolutely entitled to the assets of the trust [101].

(2) Any power of investment including the general power of investment and any power conferred by the trust instrument must be exercised in accordance with the Standard Investment Criteria, namely the suitability of the investments and the need for diversification [102].

(3) Trustees must further review the trust investments from time to time and consider whether in the light of the Standard Investment Criteria they should be varied [103].

(4) Before exercising any power of investment or reviewing investments, trustees must obtain and consider proper advice about the way in which, in accordance with the Standard Investment Criteria, the powers should be exercised unless the trustees reasonably conclude that in all the circumstances it is unnecessary or inappropriate for them to do so [104].

(5) The general power of investment applies to trusts whether created before or after the commencement of the Act and is conferred in addition to any other powers which the trustees may have but subject to any restrictions or exclusions imposed by the trust instrument (except

---

100 For example, a trustee who is guilty of self-dealing, such as under the rule in *Keech v Sandford* (1726) 2 Eq Cas Abr 741.
101 See para **3.11**.
102 See para **3.23**.
103 See para **3.25**.
104 See para **3.32**.

in the case of trust instruments made before 3 August 1961, which will not restrict or exclude the Act) [105].

(6) Trustees exercising the general power of investment and carrying out their duties to observe the Standard Investment Criteria and to seek proper advice are subject to the statutory duty of care, insofar as it applies to the trust in question [106].

---

105 See para **3.56**.
106 See para **3.44**.

Chapter 4

ACQUISITION OF LAND

'The English law of real property has never achieved simplicity, which according to Lord Bryce, distinguishes the laws of more civilised ages.'[1]

INTRODUCTION

4.1 At first sight there appears to be little justification for treating the trustees' powers to acquire land under the new Act as a separate chapter from the new powers of investment. The new Act itself deals with the powers separately, on the basis that it made the consequential amendments necessary to bring the new provisions into effect easier[2].

4.2 However, there is in fact a great deal of sense in treating acquisition of land as a distinct topic from the new powers of investment. The new provisions relating to trustees' powers to acquire land have only partially to do with investment. For many trustees, the real virtue in the new provisions will be the power to acquire land for the occupation of the beneficiaries, and strictly that would not fall within the meaning of 'investment'[3].

4.3 Part III of the Act contains the new powers for trustees to acquire land. Therefore, after the commencement of the Act there will be two ways in which trustees hold land: either under the provisions of the new Act, or under the provisions of the moribund, but not yet dead, Settled Land Act 1925. The Act not only creates the new provisions, but amends the Settled Land Act 1925. Before turning to the detail of those provisions, it is useful to look at the state of the law before the commencement of the Act, to understand the aims behind the reforms, and their extent.

THE BACKGROUND TO THE REFORMS

Trusts of personalty

4.4 The anomalous position prior to the new Act, was that trustees of a settlement of personalty had no power to invest in land in the absence of an express provision in the trust deed enabling them to do so. Consequently, any trust of personal property reliant upon the Trustee Investments Act 1961 would not enable the trustees to purchase land, although mortgages of

---

1   Megarry and Wade: *Law of Real Property*, 4th edn (Sweet & Maxwell), p 1.
2   See the Law Commission's explanatory notes to the Bill in the Report at p 99.
3   *Re Power's Will Trusts* [1947] Ch 572.

either freehold land or leaseholds with more than 60 years to run were permitted[4]. The position was of course different if the trustees were pension trustees[5].

4.5 Even if a trust of personalty contained an express provision enabling investment in land, it has been long established that that would not enable the purchase of land as a residence for a beneficiary[6]. Therefore, even the widest clause enabling the trustees to invest as absolute owners would not enable them to buy a property for a beneficiary, even the life tenant, to live in as no income would be produced and it would therefore not be an investment.

Trusts of land

4.6 This position has to be contrasted with the powers of trustees under a trust of land (within the meaning of the Trusts of Land and Appointment of Trustees Act 1996 (the 1996 Act)) or under a strict settlement governed by the Settled Land Act 1925. Under such settlements, the trustees not only had power to invest in land but also to purchase land for any other purpose.

4.7 Since the coming into force of the 1996 Act, it has not been possible to create new strict settlements[7] but the 1996 Act had no effect on pre-existing settlements. It will, consequently, take some time before all strict settlements become a thing of history. Therefore, after 1996 there have been two ways in which land might be held on trust: either under a trust of land in accordance with the 1996 Act, or under a strict settlement governed by the Settled Land Act 1925.

4.8 Under a strict settlement, any capital monies arising might be invested or otherwise applied by the trustees of the settlement for one or more of the 21 purposes specified under the Settled Land Act 1925[8]. One of those purposes was for the purchase of land held in fee simple or on a lease with 60 or more years unexpired. The tenant for life could direct the way in which the capital of the settlement was invested, in default of which the trustees had the power to make the choice[9], but subject to obtaining the consent of any person required by the settlement. In altering any application or investment of the capital monies, the trustee had to obtain the consent of the

---

4   Trustee Investments Act 1961, Sch 1, Part II, para 13.
5   Where they could rely upon their powers to invest as if absolute owners under s 34(1) of the Pensions Act 1995.
6   *Re Power's Will Trusts* [1947] Ch 572. The Law Commission's Consultation Paper No 146 'Trustees' Powers and Duties' accepted that this decision, although subject to serious question, nevertheless represented the law (para 8.5).
7   Section 2(1) of the Trusts of Land and Appointment of Trustees Act 1996.
8   Section 73(1) of the Settled Land Act 1925.
9   Section 75(2) of the Settled Land Act 1925.

tenant for life while his beneficial interest subsisted[10]. If the tenant for life exercised these powers, he did so as trustee[11]. If the land (or indeed heirlooms) subject to a strict settlement are sold, and there is no property remaining subject to the settlement, the 1996 Act provides that the settlement comes to an end[12]. Thereafter the trust property becomes subject to the provisions of the 1996 Act which are discussed below.

4.9 Land not held under a trust governed by the Settled Land Act 1925, is now held as a trust of land[13]. All trusts where land is held which were created after the commencement of the 1996 Act[14] are trusts of land. Trustees of land had for the purpose of exercising their functions as trustees all the powers of an absolute owner of the land[15]. Moreover, they were expressly empowered to purchase a legal estate in any land in England and Wales by way of investment, for the occupation by any beneficiary, or for any other reason[16]. Therefore, the impact of the decision in *Re Power's Will Trusts* was abrogated in respect of land held on a trust of land. Furthermore, the power applied notwithstanding the fact that the trustees had sold all their land and held only the proceeds[17].

4.10 There follows a summary of the position before the coming into force of the new Act:

(1) Trustees of personalty reliant on the Trustee Investments Act 1961 had no power either to invest in land, or to purchase it for any other purpose such as the occupation of a beneficiary.

(2) In the case of a trust of personalty with a wide investment clause, but no express power to purchase a property for occupation of a beneficiary, land could be acquired only if income was produced; it could not be bought to provide a residence for a beneficiary, even the life tenant.

(3) In the case of a trust of land still governed by the Settled Land Act 1925, because it was created prior to the commencement of the 1996 Act on 1 January 1997, the tenant for life, or in default of him the trustees of the settlement, could apply capital money in the purchase of freehold land or land held on a lease with a least 60 years unexpired; this did not need to be strictly by way of investment.

---

10 Section 75(4) of the Settled Land Act 1925.
11 *Re Sir Robert Peel's Settled Estates* [1910] 1 Ch 389.
12 Section 2(4) of the 1996 Act.
13 Section 1 of the 1996 Act.
14 Ie 1 January 1997.
15 Section 6(1) of the 1996 Act.
16 Section 6(3) and (4) of the 1996 Act.
17 See s 17(1) of the 1996 Act, reversing the decision in *Re Wakeman* [1945] Ch 277.

(4) In the case of a trust of land, or a trust of the proceeds of land, the trustees had the power to purchase freehold or leasehold land of whatever type, either by way of investment, or for the occupation of a beneficiary or for any other reason.

In short, the law prior to the new Act, lacked any logic and was in clear need of reform.

THE NEW POWERS TO ACQUIRE LAND

4.11 As noted earlier [18], the general power of investment contained in s 3 of the Act does not include a power for trustees to invest in land. This is, however, conferred by s 8 of the Act which provides:

'(1)   A trustee may acquire freehold or leasehold land in the United Kingdom –
  (a)   as an investment,
  (b)   for occupation by a beneficiary, or
  (c)   for any other reason.'

The term 'acquire' is clearly wider than purchase and would enable the trustee to acquire land in other ways, for example by exchange.

4.12 The section thereafter adopts the powers given to trustees under s 6(3) and (4) of the 1996 Act for all trustees (subject to what is said below) giving them all the powers of an absolute owner. Subsections 6(3) and (4) having experienced a very short life span, were reincarnated as s 8 of the new Act.

4.13 For the purposes of this section, 'beneficiary' does not mean a person interested in the due administration of an estate, as it does elsewhere in the Act [19]. It means a person who, under the will of the deceased or under the law relating to intestacy, is beneficially interested in the estate [20]. This may at first sight appear to be a distinction without a difference. However, a person interested in the due administration of the estate of a deceased includes a creditor who can bring an administration action. It would clearly be inappropriate to include such a person as someone in whose favour the power in s 8 could be exercised. It will of course be relatively uncommon for this power to be used during the administration of an estate as opposed to after the creation of a trust set up by the will or under the intestacy.

4.14 In other respects, the Act is silent on the categories of beneficiaries in whose favour the power can be exercised. If read literally, it would seem that trustees can exercise the power in favour of any beneficiary under the trust in question. However, in the case of a trust where the trust fund is directed to

---

18   See para **3.13**.
19   Section 35(2)(b).
20   Section 35(2)(c).

be held for A for life, remainder to B, can a house be purchased for B to live in? The answer would seem to be a clear 'no', as the trustees would be altering the beneficial interests in the trust, by exercising an administrative power. Moreover, they would be in clear breach of their duty to hold the balance between the tenant for life and the remainderman. On the other hand, there would seem to be no reason why the trustees could not exercise the power in favour of any beneficiary under a discretionary trust or an accumulation and maintenance trust[21].

4.15 'Freehold or leasehold land' is defined as a legal estate in land[22]. The effect of this is that trustees cannot invest in equitable interests in land, nor can they invest in other legal interests in land such as rentcharges[23]. The general power of investment does not permit a trustee to make investments in land[24] other than loans secured on land, or in accordance with s 8[25]. Section 8 only enables a trustee to acquire a legal estate in land. Therefore, if trustees were offered the chance to acquire a beneficial interest in, say, a commercial property, which might provide a very good return, they would be unable to do so under these new statutory powers of investment. This appears to be a serious lacuna.

4.16 However, the new Act does solve one problem. Without an express power in the trust instrument, trustees could not hold property jointly or in common with other persons on the basis that it is the duty of the trustees to take control of the trust property[26]. By providing the trustees with the powers of an absolute owner, the general power of investment resolves this difficulty. Clearly, this will have ramifications in relation to other types of property, but may be particularly important in respect of land.

4.17 The power contained in s 8 is confined to land in the UK. This is perhaps rather too narrow in the light of the current global economy. Many trustees hold land in other jurisdictions, particularly if there are beneficiaries resident there, or some other connection between the trust and that country. The reasoning behind the confinement of the power to the UK is

---

21 Although a careful eye has to be kept on whether the beneficiary would be treated by the Revenue as having an interest in possession for inheritance tax purposes thereafter.

22 Section 8(2).

23 Interestingly permitted by the Trustee Investments Act 1961, and in respect of trustees who have invested in perpetual rentcharges before the coming into force of the Act, they will not be regarded as exceeding their powers of investment just because they retain those rentcharges, see para 7 of Sch 3 to the Act.

24 Which is not defined in the Act but which for the purposes must be presumed to be defined as in the Interpretation Act 1978 as 'buildings and other structures, land covered with water; and any estate, interest easement, servitude or right in or over land'. The Act does not adopt the definition in s 205 of the Law of Property Act 1925.

25 Section 3(3).

26 *Webb v Jonas* (1888) 39 Ch D 660.

that the law relating to real property is governed by where that real property is situated, its lex situs[27]. Moreover, not all jurisdictions recognise the concept of a trust and provide the same protection for beneficiaries which apply in the UK[28].

4.18   While there is considerable force in these arguments, there seems little sense in choosing the jurisdictions of the UK, rather than listing certain countries which do recognise trusts such as those which have ratified the Hague Convention on Trusts and where there would be little difficulty in the beneficiaries being protected.

4.19   It is possible that in jurisdictions where equitable interests in land are not regarded as land as such[29], trustees will be able to invest in those interests in land by relying on the general power of investment.

POWERS OF THE TRUSTEES ONCE LAND HAS BEEN ACQUIRED

4.20   Trustees of land have since the commencement of the 1996 Act enjoyed all the powers of an absolute owner for the purposes of carrying out their functions as trustees[30]. Trustees of personalty, even if they had an express power to invest in land, did not (until they then become trustees of land) have such powers, and perhaps most notably the power to acquire it by way of mortgage.

4.21   The new Act adopts the provisions of the 1996 Act in respect of trusts of personalty or trusts of land (but not trustees of strict settlements) and confers on a trustee who acquires land all the powers of an absolute owner in relation to the land[31]. Therefore, having acquired the land, trustees will be able, for example, to lease it, carry out repairs and improvements to it, and mortgage it. For some settlors or testators, this power may appear too wide, and in some circumstances it may be desirable to cut it down. Notwithstanding the fact that the power is so wide, it is of course subject to the general trust principles that the trustees must act in the best interests of the beneficiaries, and, as set out below, observe the statutory duty of care.

---

27   Recognition of trusts is governed by the Hague Convention on the Law Applicable to Trusts (incorporated into English law by the Recognition of Trusts Act 1987).
28   See the Report at para 2.42 and the notes thereto.
29   As was the case prior to the abolition of the doctrine of conversion in this jurisdiction.
30   Section 6(1) of the 1996 Act.
31   Section 8(3) of the Act.

DUTY OF CARE

4.22 The statutory duty of care applies to the exercise by the trustees of their power to acquire land under s 8[32] and any other similar power whether conferred by the trust instrument or in any other manner[33]. It further applies to the exercise of any power in relation to that land once acquired[34], whether those are powers conferred by the trust instrument, or the powers contained in s 8(3) of the Act.

4.23 This of course provides a welcome safeguard, and ensures that trustees must exercise proper care and skill in deciding whether or not to acquire land in the first place and then in managing that land when they have it. The duty of care can (as discussed elsewhere) be excluded by the trust instrument[35].

4.24 It is notable that while all the other provisions of s 6 of the 1996 Act were in effect re-enacted in s 8 of the new Act, s 6(5) was not. This provided that the trustees must have regard to the rights of the beneficiaries in exercising their powers under s 6. The explanatory notes to the Bill indicated that, notwithstanding the failure to re-enact this provision, it was not intended to cut down the duties of the trustees. As a matter of general law, it seems clear that the trustees must exercise their powers in the interests of the beneficiaries, and perhaps s 6(5) was simply otiose.

SCOPE OF THE POWER

4.25 The power in s 8 is in addition to powers conferred on trustees otherwise than by Part III of the Act[36]. Therefore if, as is quite commonly the case, the trust instrument contains an express power for the trustees to invest in land, but no power to purchase a property in which a beneficiary can live, the new Act will supplement that.

4.26 On the other hand, the new statutory power is subject to any restriction or exclusion imposed by the trust instrument, or by any enactment or any provision of subordinate legislation[37]. Therefore, in trust instruments created prior to the commencement of the Act, a provision that expressly prohibited the trustees from investing in land would exclude the powers conferred in s 8 at least partially. In respect of this part of the Act, there is no provision that trusts made prior to 3 August 1961 cannot exclude

---

32 Paragraph 2(a) of Sch 1 to the Act.
33 Paragraph 2(b) of Sch 1 to the Act.
34 Paragraph 2(c) of Sch 1 to the Act.
35 Paragraph 5 of Sch 1 to the Act.
36 Section 9(a).
37 Section 9(b).

these provisions. In trusts created after the commencement of the Act, it will, where appropriate, be possible to exclude the operation of the section[38].

4.27   Part III of the Act relating to the acquisition of land neither applies to strict settlements[39] nor to trusts to which the Universities and College Estates Act 1925 applies[40]. The latter Act provides a statutory code similar to the powers conferred on a tenant for life under the Settled Land Act 1925 for certain universities[41]. It also does not apply to trustees of an occupational pension scheme[42], trustees of authorised unit trusts[43], or a common investment scheme or common deposit scheme made under the Charities Act 1993[44].

4.28   Subject to these exclusions, Part III applies in relation to trusts whether created before or after its commencement[45].

STRICT SETTLEMENTS

4.29   Part III of the Act does not apply to a trust of property which consists of or includes land but which (despite s 2 of the 1996 Act) is settled land[46]. In other words, strict settlements in existence on 1 January 1997, and still subsisting, will be unaffected by the new powers conferred in s 8 of the Act. Therefore, the power to invest capital arising under a strict settlement will still depend on s 73 of the Settled Land Act 1925, and therefore there is power to apply capital in the acquisition of freehold land and leases with more than 60 years left unexpired.

4.30   The strict settlement does not come out of the Act completely unscathed. There are in fact some far-reaching changes made to the way in which the powers to apply capital money operate, which in the light of their importance to the nature of strict settlements are somewhat surprisingly to be found tucked away in the consequential amendments made as a result of the reforms introduced by the new Act[47].

---

38   See the precedent for the clause: form D at Appendix III.
39   Which are dealt with in more detail below as the Settled Land Act 1925 is substantially amended by the new Act, and this appeared a convenient place to deal with it.
40   Section 10(1)(a) and (b).
41   Oxford, Cambridge and Durham.
42   Section 36(3).
43   Section 37. An 'authorised unit trust' means a unit trust in the case of which an order under s 78 of the Financial Services Act 1986 is in force.
44   Section 38, and see ss 24 and 25 of the Charities Act 1993.
45   Section 10(2).
46   Section 10(1) of the Act.
47   Paragraphs 5 to 15 of Sch 2.

4.31 The first major change is that the investment or other application of capital monies is no longer to be at the direction of the tenant for life, and in default according to the discretion of the trustees. Instead, the discretion as to how the trust fund should be invested is vested in the trustees, and any investment is to be in the names or under the control of the trustees[48]. This is a radical departure from the principles underpinning the Settled Land Act 1925, whereby the tenant for life managed the settled land and its proceeds. Furthermore, the requirement that the consent of the tenant for life must be obtained before any investment or application of capital monies was altered during the currency of his beneficial interest, has been dispensed with. Instead, the trustees in exercising their power to invest or apply capital money, 'shall (a) so far as practical, consult the tenant for life; and (b) so far as consistent with the general interest of the settlement give effect to his wishes'[49]. This mirrors the requirement in the 1996 Act for the beneficiaries to be consulted by the trustees[50]. It is clearly a considerable watering down of the requirement that the trustees could not alter the investment of capital monies without the consent of the tenant for life. Although he must be consulted (so far as practical), his wishes can be ignored, provided that the trustees can say that it was not in the general interest of the trust to comply with those wishes. The consent of the tenant for life is still required during the subsistence of his beneficial interest, if the trustees wish to alter the application or investment of monies under the direction of the court[51].

4.32 Clearly, problems could arise if the trustees delegated their investment powers under s 11 of the Act[52], and the tenant for life was not consulted by the agent. New provisions are therefore inserted into the Settled Land Act 1925 which provide that the trustees may not delegate their functions in such a way that they are prevented from complying with their obligations under s 75(4) to consult the tenant for life[53]. Furthermore, a new subs 75(4C) provides that anyone authorised to exercise the trustees' functions under s 11, with respect to the application or investment of capital money, will not be subject to the obligation to consult the tenant for life and give effect to his wishes. Therefore, the trustees must ensure that they remain in a position to carry out any consultation required by s 75(4), notwithstanding the delegation of their functions to an agent. This is likely to prove cumbersome in practice. One of the advantages of delegation under the new

---

48   Section 75(2) of the Settled Land Act 1925, as amended by para 8(1) of Sch 2 to the Act.

49   Section 75(4) of the Settled Land Act 1925, as amended by the Act.

50   Section 11(1).

51   Section 75(4A) of the Settled Land Act 1925, inserted by para 8(2) of Sch 2 to the Act.

52   As to which, see Chapter 3 above.

53   Section 75(4B) of the Settled Land Act 1925, and for a clause to insert into terms of appointment of an agent, see Appendix III.

Act, is that the trustees can hand over their investment powers to someone with the expertise to handle them, and can then concentrate on other matters in relation to the trust fund. Where there is a strict settlement, the trustees will have to remain involved in all investment decisions if only to the extent of consulting the tenant for life and deciding whether it is in the general interest of the settlement to follow his wishes. In essence, it appears that trustees of a strict settlement cannot delegate their investment powers on a fully discretionary basis.

4.33 It is understood that one of the reasons for this radical departure in the way in which strict settlements operate, was that it was considered that the new powers of delegation conferred by the Act would lead to great difficulties if the investment functions under a strict settlement were divided between the tenant for life and the trustees. Both might delegate. This appears unconvincing, as restrictions could have been placed on who could delegate and when. For those practitioners who dislike strict settlements, and cannot wait to see their passing, this latest body blow to the already terminally sick strict settlement will no doubt be welcomed. For those of us who mourn their passing, it is less welcome.

4.34 Nothing in the amendments made to s 75 of the Settled Land Act 1925 by the new Act affects any directions given to the trustees before the commencement of para 8 of Sch 2 to the Act, by the tenant for life but not yet acted upon [54].

4.35 A further amendment made to the Settled Land Act 1925 is the insertion of a new section 75A [55], which enables the tenant for life or statutory owner where land subject to the settlement is sold for an estate in fee simple or for a lease having at least 500 years to run, and the proceeds are liable to be invested, with the consent of the trustees to contract that the payment of any part of the purchase price shall remain outstanding and be secured by a charge by way of legal mortgage or the land sold with or without the security of any other property [56]. This new provision is based closely on s 10(2) of the Trustee Act 1925 which is repealed by the Act, and clearly provides tenants for life and statutory owners with a useful power.

4.36 The power is subject to certain terms. If any buildings are comprised on the land, the legal charge must contain a covenant by the mortgagor to keep them insured for their full value against loss or damage due to any event [57]. The tenant for life or statutory owner exercising the power under this new section, or the trustees giving their consent to the exercise of that power, do not have to seek proper advice under s 5 of the Act, nor is he liable

---

54   Paragraph 8(3) of Sch 2 to the Act.
55   Paragraph 9 of Sch 2 to the Act.
56   Section 75A(1) of the Settled Land Act 1925.
57   Ibid, s 75A(2).

for any loss incurred merely because the security is insufficient at the date of the charge[58]. If there is anyone specified in the trust instrument whose consent is required to a change of investment, they must consent to the exercise of this power[59]. Where the sale is one which has been ordered by the court, the power will be available only if and so far as the court may by order direct[60]. This is something which ought to be borne very much in mind when making applications involving an order for the sale of settled property, and in drafting those orders.

SUMMARY

4.37   There follows a summary of the provisions relating to the acquisition of land.

(1) Trustees now have the power to acquire the legal estate in freehold and leasehold land in the UK either as an investment, for occupation by a beneficiary or for any other reason[61].

(2) Once land has been acquired, trustees have all the powers of an absolute owner in respect of the land[62].

(3) These powers are in addition to any other powers conferred by the trust instrument or otherwise but subject to any restrictions or exclusions in the trust instrument[63].

(4) In exercising these powers, the trustees are subject to the statutory duty of care insofar as no contrary intention is shown in the trust instrument[64].

(5) The powers apply to trusts whether created before or after the commencement of Part III of the Act[65].

(6) The provisions do not apply to land still subject to the Settled Land Act 1925 regime nor to land held subject to the Universities and College Estates Act 1925[66].

(7) Powers of investment under the Settled Land Act 1925 will henceforth be exercisable by the trustees of the settlement rather than the tenant for life[67].

---

58   Section 75A(3) of the Settled Land Act 1925.
59   Ibid, s 75A(4).
60   Ibid, s 75A(5).
61   See para **4.11**.
62   See para **4.20**.
63   See para **4.22**.
64   See para **4.25**.
65   Ibid.
66   Ibid.
67   See para **4.29**.

Chapter 5

AGENTS, CUSTODIANS AND NOMINEES

'When in charge, ponder. When in trouble, delegate . . .'[1]

INTRODUCTION

5.1 One of the main reasons for the enactment of the Trustee Act 2000 ('the Act') was the general dissatisfaction with the law concerning the use of agents, custodians and nominees by trustees. At para 4.6 of the Report[2], the Law Commission gave its view on the pre-Act position:

> 'In the Law Commission's view, the deficiencies in the present law are not as to when trustees may delegate, but as to what they may delegate. Indeed, the Commission took the same view in the Consultation Paper. Whilst certain limitations on trustees' powers of delegation are wholly appropriate, others now constitute a serious impediment to the administration of trusts.'

5.2 It should be noted from the outset that the form of delegation being dealt with by the Law Commission's Report (and as a consequence, the Act) is *collective* delegation by the trustees as a body, as opposed to *individual* delegation by each trustee[3].

SUMMARY OF OLD LAW

5.3 Under the law prior to the passing of the Act, trustees were given limited powers to appoint agents by virtue of s 23(1) and (3) of the Trustee Act 1925 ('the 1925 Act'). These powers were extremely limited. Trustees could employ agents to 'transact any business or do any act required to be transacted or done in the execution of the trust'[4]; appoint agents to carry out all of their functions in respect of property outside the UK[5]; when selling land, appoint a solicitor to receive purchase money and give a good discharge for it[6]; and to delegate to either a banker or a solicitor the power to

---

1   James H Boren, *New York Times*, 8 November 1970.
2   Law Com No 260.
3   The latter form of delegation was the subject of reform by the Trustee Delegation Act 1999.
4   Trustee Act 1925, s 23(1).
5   Ibid, s 23(2).
6   Ibid, s 23(3)(a). This provision was subject to the qualification that the trustees had to have signed a receipt for the money.

receive and give a good discharge for the proceeds under an insurance policy[7].

5.4 The delegation provisions under the 1925 Act were open to criticism for a number of reasons[8], but the main complaint (as highlighted by the extract quoted at para **5.1**) was that the limited permissible scope of collective delegation was a serious impediment to the effective administration of a trust. This was due to the principle that a trustee was able only to delegate ministerial, and not fiduciary functions, coupled with the designation of the power of choosing investments as fiduciary[9]. As a result, whilst it was possible to instruct an agent to carry out a particular investment transaction chosen by the trustees, it was not possible to permit the agent to make the choice of the investment himself. Thus trusts incorporating the default provisions under the 1925 Act have been unable to take full advantage of the services of fund managers and the like.

5.5 Similarly, only limited powers existed in relation to the use of custodians and nominees. Section 21 of the 1925 Act permitted trustees to deposit documents with bankers and the like; and s 7(1) required the deposit of bearer securities with a banker or banking company. In addition, provision was made under the Public Trustee Act 1906, s 4 for the appointment of 'custodian trustees'.

5.6 Thus, wholesale reform of this area was both overdue and extremely welcome. As well as widening the powers to use agents, custodians and nominees, the Act has made a considerable advance in seeking to provide a comprehensive code for their appointment and supervision, and in treating agents, custodians and nominees all in a similar way, something which could not be said of the 1925 Act.

THE NEW REGIME

5.7 For the first time, there is a comprehensive and cohesive code governing the appointment of agents, nominees and custodians by trustees. The provisions are contained in Part IV of the Act. The new rules apply to trusts created both before and after commencement of the Act[10], and are in addition to any powers conferred otherwise than by the Act[11]; and are subject to any restrictions imposed by the trust instrument or any other legislation[12].

---

7   Trustee Act 1925, s 23(3)(c).
8   See Law Com Consultation Paper No 146, Part III.
9   See *Rowland v Witherden* (1851) 3 Mac & G 568.
10   Trustee Act 2000, s 27.
11   Ibid, s 26(a).
12   Ibid, s 26(b).

5.8 The Act gives the tenant for life under a Settled Land Act 1925 settlement the power to appoint agents, but not custodians or nominees [13]. Therefore, ss 11, 13 to 15 and 21 to 23 and 32 apply in this context. Notable is the omission of s 12, which prevents a beneficiary from being appointed as an agent [14], therefore in relation to a strict settlement, a beneficiary may be appointed by the life tenant as agent. This makes perfect sense, as it is a beneficiary who already has the power being delegated, and it would therefore be curious for that beneficiary to have no power to delegate to another. These exceptions should be borne in mind when reading the following paragraphs.

AGENTS

5.9 Section 11 of the Act contains a general power to trustees to appoint agents. Under the new power, trustees (whether charitable or non-charitable) may delegate to an agent any or all of what are described as 'delegable functions' [15].

5.10 The Act thereafter draws a distinction between charitable and non-charitable trustees. It does so by providing different definitions of 'delegable functions' for each. For non-charitable trustees, 'delegable functions' means any function other than: (a) any function relating to whether or in what way trust assets should be distributed [16]; (b) any power to decide whether any fees or payments should be made out of the income or capital of the trust fund [17]; (c) any power to appoint trustees [18]; and (d) any power to delegate to an agent or to appoint a nominee or custodian [19].

5.11 The functions listed in s 11(2) and thereby excluded from the scope of the power to delegate are those which are clearly inappropriate for exercise by anyone other than the appointed trustees. Both the power to distribute assets or to decide whether to make payments from income or capital have an important bearing on the rights and interest of the beneficiaries under the trust. Such decisions are of a clear, fiduciary nature, go to the very heart of trusteeship, and therefore should be exercised by the persons occupying the office of trustee, and not their delegate.

5.12 The functions which are capable of being delegated are, in the main, ministerial in nature, but crucially (and unlike under the 1925 Act), the

---

13 Schedule 2, para 17.
14 See para **5.16**.
15 Section 11(1).
16 Section 11(2)(a).
17 Section 11(2)(b).
18 Section 11(2)(c).
19 Section 11(2)(d).

agent can be given some discretion as to the way in which he exercises the powers given to him, rather than merely carrying out the trustees' instructions. For example, an agent may now decide to acquire and/or sell land, rather than merely carrying out the trustees' instructions to do so. Most importantly, trustees may now appoint a fund manager to manage the trust's investment portfolio, and thereby (hopefully) maximise the return on investment for the beneficiaries[20].

5.13 The approach towards delegation by charitable trustees is different. The definition of 'delegable functions' for charitable trustees is much narrower than that for their non-charitable counterparts. Instead of being able to delegate any functions not specifically excluded by the statute, charitable trustees may delegate only the functions set out in s 11(3). These are as follows:

(a) any function consisting of carrying out a decision taken by the trustees[21];
(b) any function relating to the management of investments (including dealing with land where it is held as an investment)[22]; and
(c) any function relating to fund raising other than by means of a profit of a trade which forms 'an integral part of carrying out the trust's charitable purpose'[23].

In addition, power is given to the Secretary of State to add to the list of charitable trustees' delegable functions by order[24].

5.14 As noted above, s 11(3)(c) excludes from the definition of delegable functions which relate to raising of funds, but which are an integral part of the carrying out of the trust's charitable purpose. A more detailed explanation of what is meant by the term is set out in s 11(4), which provides that a trade is an integral part of the trust's charitable purpose if:

(a) the profits are applied solely to the purposes of the trust; and either
(b) the trade is carried out in the course of the actual carrying out of a primary purpose of the trust[25]; or
(c) the work in connection with the trade is mainly carried out by beneficiaries of the trust[26].

---

20   See para **5.25** for the additional requirements in relation to the delegation of asset management functions.
21   Section 11(3)(a).
22   Section 11(3)(b).
23   Section 11(3)(c).
24   Section 11(3)(d).
25   Section 11(4)(a).
26   Section s 11(4)(b).

An example of such a trade would be, say, one which is for the purpose of providing jobs for disabled people and operated by a charity with the employment of disabled people as one of its objects. In such circumstances, it would not be possible for the trustees to delegate functions in relation to that trade.

5.15 The reason for differentiation between charitable and non-charitable trusts given by the Law Commission[27] is that, in the context of a charitable trust, it is more difficult to distinguish between the functions which should and should not be delegable, as the concept of 'charitable purposes' in general law is wider than the objects for which charitable trusts exist. Thus if the line were to be drawn between charitable functions (non-delegable) and non-charitable (delegable), a number of functions which it would be desirable to permit trustees to delegate would be excluded from the category of delegable functions. Examples given are: donations of surplus funds to other charities, reinvestment of surplus income and payments made for administrative purposes. Therefore, the Act has been drafted in such a way as to spell out exactly what may be delegated, with provision for the Secretary of State to add to the list by order should the current list of delegable functions be found to be inadequate.

Whom may the trustees appoint as an agent?

5.16 The Act gives a wide discretion to trustees in respect of whom they may appoint to act as agent. Trustees may not appoint a beneficiary to act as their agent, even if that person is also a trustee[28]. However, apart from that, it would seem that practically anyone is eligible for appointment, including a person already appointed as a nominee or custodian[29] or one of the trustees (provided he is not a beneficiary). The only additional limitation is that the trustees may not authorise two or more people to carry out the same function unless they are to exercise the function jointly[30].

Terms of agency

5.17 Section 14 of the Act sets out certain requirements in relation to the terms upon which agents should (and should not) be engaged. In general, trustees have a wide discretion as to the terms upon which they may engage a person to act as their agent, the Act providing that subject to certain exceptions[31] they may appoint a person as their agent 'on such terms as to remuneration and other matters as they may determine'[32]. The exercise of this wide discretion is subject to the statutory duty of care[33].

---

27 At para 4.38 of the Report, and para 6.62 of the Consultation Document.
28 Section 12(3). This does not apply to strict settlements, see para **5.8**.
29 Section 12(4).
30 Section 12(2).
31 Set out in ss 14(2), 15(2), and 29 to 32.
32 Section 14(1).
33 Schedule 1, para 3(1). See para **2.19**.

5.18 Trustees are not, however, permitted to incorporate terms which either:

(a) permit the agent to appoint a substitute [34];
(b) restrict the liability of the agent (or substitute) to the trustees or any beneficiary [35]; or
(c) permit the agent to act in circumstances giving rise to a conflict of interest [36]

unless the inclusion of such a term is 'reasonably necessary' [37].

No attempt is made by the Act to explain in what circumstances the inclusion of any of the terms mentioned above will fall into the 'reasonably necessary' category, but essentially this will be a question of fact in each case. Presumably, if it is normal for, say, investment managers to accept an engagement on terms with restricted liability (and unlikely for them to accept an appointment without such a term), it will be 'reasonably necessary' to restrict liability *if* the use of an investment manager can be shown to be in the best interests of the trust. It may seem surprising to some readers that it is contemplated that the appointment of an agent upon terms which permit him to act in circumstances where a conflict of interest may arise could be 'reasonably necessary'. However, this is geared towards a particular situation: the appointment of an investment manager who is also a market-maker. In that case, there is a possibility that the investment manager will be self-dealing.

5.19 If it can be shown that the trustees have included such terms where they were not 'reasonably necessary', the beneficiaries will be able to bring an action for breach of the statutory duty of care to recover any loss caused [38].

5.20 An agent, custodian or nominee appointed by the trustees may, of course, be paid for his services. Where an agent, custodian or nominee is appointed, and that person is not a trustee, the trustees may remunerate him out of the trust fund for the services provided if:

(a) the terms of engagement permit such remuneration for those services [39]; and
(b) the amount is 'reasonable' [40].

In addition, agents, custodians and nominees may be reimbursed out of the

---

34   Section 14(3)(a).
35   Section 14(3)(b).
36   Section 14(3)(c).
37   Section 14(2).
38   See Chapter 2 above.
39   Section 32(2)(a).
40   Section 32(2)(b).

trust fund for expenses properly incurred in exercising the functions of agent, custodian or nominee[41].

5.21 The reasonable rate of remuneration is likely to be determined by reference to the 'going rate' in the market. Where trustees are able to negotiate rates of remuneration with a particular agent, custodian or nominee, they should endeavour to collect a range of the fees charged in the marketplace for the services to be provided. A failure to do so may result in too high a level of fees being agreed, and the possibility of a claim by the beneficiaries for a breach of the statutory duty of care. Similarly, where an agent, custodian or nominee has a fixed scale of fees (as will often be the case), trustees should ensure that they 'shop around' and consider whether the potentially higher rates of remuneration demanded by their preferred appointee can be justified in some way (eg by a better performance in the investment markets over a certain period). Again, by trustees choosing a more expensive agent, custodian or nominee without having some tangible reason for doing so, the beneficiaries will be entitled to feel aggrieved and are likely to bring a claim for breach of the statutory duty of care.

5.22 It is interesting to note that the Act does not require sums reimbursed to agents, custodians or nominees to be reasonable in amount, merely properly incurred. It would seem, therefore, that provided the nature of the expense is shown to be justified, the amount thereof need not be. Notwithstanding this, trustees would be well advised to seek, where possible, to incorporate into an agent, custodian or nominee's terms of engagement that expenses to be reimbursed from the trust fund be shown to be reasonable in amount in order to minimise claims from beneficiaries aggrieved by an agent, custodian or nominee being given carte blanche to run up expenses.

5.23 The remuneration of trustees appointed as agents, custodians or nominees is governed by ss 29(6)[42] and 30(2)[43]. The rules governing the remuneration of trustees are dealt with in Chapter 6 below.

5.24 Trustees acting as agent, custodian or nominee may also be reimbursed for their expenses properly incurred when acting on behalf of the trust[44]. However, the points raised at para **5.22** are of particular importance when trustees are to be appointed as agent, custodian or nominee so as to avoid any accusation that trustees are acting in their own interests in incurring considerable levels of expenses, even though the type of expense is perfectly proper.

---

41   Section 32(3).
42   For trustees of non-charitable trusts.
43   For trustees of charitable trusts.
44   Section 31(2).

Asset management

5.25 Further requirements are imposed where trustees seek to delegate their 'asset management functions'[45]. Trustees may authorise a person to exercise their asset management functions only by way of an agreement made or evidenced in writing[46]. Further, they must also prepare a 'policy statement'[47] which provides guidance as to how the functions should be exercised[48] and ensure that the terms of appointment require the agent to secure compliance with the statement[49] or any revised or amended version of it[50]. The guidance given by the trustees in the policy statement must be formulated with a view to ensuring that the functions delegated will be exercised in the best interests of the trust[51]. Although this term is not defined, it is submitted that the courts will have no great difficulty in deciding upon whether a particular exercise of a function is in the best interests of the trust or not. A checklist of factors to be considered when entering into an asset management agreement and preparing a policy statement can be found as form M at Appendix III.

Agents' duties

5.26 An agent appointed by trustees will be subject to all the usual duties imposed upon an agent by the law of agency[52]. However, the Act imposes further specific duties upon agents appointed by use of the powers under s 11. Most importantly, where a function is delegated to an agent, the agent is subject to any duty which is 'attached' to the function[53]. Perhaps, due to the lack of clarity inherent in the use of such a term, the Act provides an example of a duty which is 'attached' to a delegable function: where an agent is authorised under s 11 to exercise the general power of investment under s 3, he is subject to the duties imposed by s 4 in relation to it[54]. An exception to this rule is that an agent is not under an obligation to obtain advice in respect

---

45 Section 15(5) defines the asset management functions of the trustees as being their functions relating to: (a) the investment of assets subject to the trust; (b) the acquisition of property which is to be subject to the trust; and (c) managing property which is subject to the trust and disposing of, or creating an interest in, such property.

46 Section 15(1).

47 Which, by virtue of s 15(4), must also be made or evidenced in writing.

48 Section 15(2)(a).

49 Section 15(2)(b)(i).

50 Section 15(2)(b)(ii).

51 Section 15(3).

52 A discussion of these duties is outside the scope of this book, however readers interested in this subject are advised to consult a specialist textbook in this field, such as *Bowstead and Reynolds on Agency*, 16th edn (Sweet & Maxwell, 1996).

53 Section 13(1).

54 Namely, to have regard to the Standard Investment Criteria and to review the investments. For a more detailed discussion of these duties, see Chapter 3 above.

of investments[55] if he is the kind of person from whom it would be proper for the trustees to obtain advice in compliance with the requirement[56].

5.27 One crucial point to note is the potential conflict between the provisions of s 14 and those of s 13(1). Section 13(1) provides that the person to whom a function is delegated is subject to the duties attached 'whatever the terms of the agency', giving the impression that duties which attach to the function delegated cannot be excluded. However, s 14 states that the agent's liability may be restricted if it is 'reasonably necessary' to do so. Perhaps one way in which the provisions can be reconciled is that the duty will automatically pass with the delegated function and cannot be excluded per se, but that liability for breach of that duty can be restricted. If this is correct, it is not particularly satisfactory, as the result is that the proviso in s 13(1) adds little (if anything) if liability for breach of the duty can be excluded under s 14. What will be interesting is whether the courts will accept the agent being indemnified by the trust for breaches of the duties to which he is subject under s 13. It could be argued that to allow such would negate the purpose of that section, effectively permitting the agent to act free from the duties imposed upon him[57].

5.28 A further difficulty is that despite the example given in subs (1), the meaning of s 13 is, to a great extent, unclear. Whilst there is no doubt that an agent to whom investment functions are delegated will be subject to the duties under ss 4 and 5 of the Act, it is not clear whether the agent will owe any fiduciary duties to the beneficiaries on whose behalf he acts.

5.29 The situation of most importance is as follows. A trustee 'T' delegates his investment management functions to an agent 'A'. T complies with his obligations to set out A's terms of engagement, setting out a clear investment policy for A to adhere to. Included in that policy is a statement that A must act fairly as between the life tenant 'L' and the remainderman 'R', T having determined the appropriate balance[58]. This mirrors T's fiduciary duty to act fairly. If A purchases a long-term investment with considerable capital growth but minimal income, he may have failed to act fairly as between L and R. A may be in breach of a duty of care owed to L at common law[59], and an action in damages is therefore a possibility in that regard. However, had T failed to act fairly as between L and R, he would have been in breach of his

---

55   Under s 5.
56   Section 13(2).
57   Of course, it may be that if an agent were to breach any such duty deliberately in the knowledge that he is protected by a term excluding liability or indemnifying him from the trust fund, he will be acting dishonestly, and thereby lose the protection afforded by any such term, see *Armitage v Nurse* [1998] Ch 241.
58   In the authors' view, trustees should determine the actual balance rather than instruct the agent to act fairly, as the decision is one of crucial importance.
59   The position is far from clear as the leading authorities on this point are in conflict, see *Carr-Glynn v Frearsons* [1999] Ch 326 and *Worby v Rosser* [2000] PNLR 140, CA.

fiduciary duty to act in such a way, and therefore liable to reconstitute the trust fund, reflecting the fair balance between income and capital[60]. However, where T has delegated in accordance with the provisions of the Act and fulfilled his duty of care, there is unlikely to be any scope for alleging unfairness as against him. Therefore, unless any fiduciary duty to act fairly can be imputed to A, L would seem to have lost the possibility of bringing any claim in equity. It is therefore essential to consider whether such a duty is owed by A to L, whether by virtue of s 13 or otherwise.

5.30   Accordingly, it must be determined whether s 13 can be construed so as to impose a fiduciary duty upon A where the investment functions have been delegated to him. Essentially, there is one question to be answered in this regard: is the duty to act fairly between beneficiaries 'attached to the function' of investing trust assets? Unfortunately, the Act gives no guidance in this regard. In principle, there is no reason why it could not be argued that, for example, the duty to act fairly as between beneficiaries could 'attach' to the investment function delegated under the Act. Indeed, it would seem appropriate in a situation where the duty is set out in the agent's instructions, and he is aware of the existence of the two different classes of beneficiary and their competing interests.

5.31   However, the contrary argument also has some force. It is that a trustee is under two distinct duties in such a situation:

(1)   a duty to invest; and
(2)   a general duty to act fairly as between the beneficiaries in all aspects of the administration of the trust, and that the balance to be struck between life tenant and remainderman in choosing investments is a result of the intersection between those two distinct duties.

As a consequence, the duty to act fairly does not attach to the investment function, but to the office and role of trustee, and therefore does not pass down to the agent by virtue of s 13.

5.32   In the authors' view, the correct construction of s 13 is the former, and accordingly an agent to whom investment functions are delegated is under a fiduciary duty to act fairly as between beneficiaries. Of assistance in this respect is the example provided in s 13(1). The duty under s 4 (the subject of the example) is not drafted in terms which could be said to attach it to the function rather than to the trustee, and in that way it is similar to the

---

60   Whether this makes any practical difference is a matter of some debate. In *Bristol & West Building Society v Mothew* [1998] Ch 1, Millett LJ (as he then was) asserted, albeit *obiter*, that the common law principles of causation and remoteness should be applied by analogy to equitable compensation, and as a consequence the quantum will be the same in both cases. However, crucial distinctions remain, as highlighted by Nicholas Warren QC: 'Trustee risk and liability' (1999) *Trust Law International*, Vol 13, No 4 at pp 230–231.

fiduciary duties to which trustees are subject. Accordingly, by using s 4 as an example of a duty attached to the investment function, 'attached to the function' in the context of s 13(1) is, in effect, being construed as meaning 'to which the trustee is subject in the exercise of the function'. Such a construction would clearly serve to pass down the trustee's fiduciary duties to the agent. Further, it is arguable that even in the absence of s 13(1) imposing the fiduciary duties upon the agent, they may be subject to them in any event[61], but the law is far from clear on this point.

5.33 Where the agent is also custodian of the investment portfolio, the 's 13(1) question' will be largely irrelevant. This is because, in such circumstances, the agent is likely to hold the assets qua trustee[62] and therefore owe a direct fiduciary duty to the beneficiaries.

5.34 The remainder of s 13 imposes specific requirements in relation to trusts to which s 11(1) of the Trusts of Land and Appointment of Trustees Act 1996 (the 1996 Act) applies[63], imposing a duty upon trustees to consult with beneficiaries. Where s 11(1) of the 1996 Act applies to a trust, trustees may not appoint an agent on terms which prevent compliance with it[64]. However, the person appointed as agent is not subject to the duty under s 11(1) of the 1996 Act[65]. Thus the trustees must ensure that consultation in accordance with s 11(1) of the 1996 Act is carried out, as there is no obligation on their agent to do so.

NOMINEES AND CUSTODIANS

5.35 Trustees may appoint nominees in relation to such of the assets of the trust as they may determine, apart from settled land[66]. Where trustees make such an appointment, they have the power to take the necessary steps to secure the vesting of the relevant assets in the nominee[67]. Any appointment of a nominee made under the powers given by the Act must be made or

---

61   See *Bordman v Phipps* [1966] 3 All ER 721, per Lord Hodson at 749C; and Consultation Document, paras 3.29 and 3.30.

62   See DJ Hayton: *Underhill and Hayton, Law of Trusts and Trustees*, 15th edn (Butterworths, 1995) at p 6.

63   That is any trust of land except: (a) a trust created by a disposition where the disposition provides that s 11 will not apply; (b) a trust created by a disposition before 1 January 1997 or a trust created after that date by reference to such a disposition; (c) a trust created by or arising under a will made before 1 January 1997 unless a deed is executed 'opting in' to the provisions. For a more detailed discussion of the provisions of s 11 of the 1996 Act, see Angela Sydenham *Trusts of Land – The New Law* (Jordans, 1996).

64   Trustee Act 2000, s 13(4).

65   Ibid, s 13(5).

66   Ibid, s 16(1)(a).

67   Ibid, s 16(1)(b).

evidenced in writing[68]. The power to use nominees is not, however, given in respect of trusts having a custodian trustee[69] or in relation to any assets vested in the official custodian for charities[70].

5.36 A custodian is defined as someone who '... undertakes the safe custody of the assets or of any documents or records concerning the assets'[71] and may be appointed by trustees by the use of the power contained in s 17 of the Act. The power given is to appoint a custodian in relation to such of the trust assets as the trustees may determine[72]. Any such appointment must be made in writing[73] and does not apply to any trust having a custodian trustee or any assets vested in the official custodian for charities[74].

5.37 These provisions are relatively straightforward: the only formality being the requirement for an agreement in writing. Restrictions upon whom may be appointed are imposed by s 19. Under that section, one of the 'relevant conditions' must be satisfied. This means that the nominee or custodian to be appointed must be either:

(a) a person whose business consists of or includes acting as a nominee or custodian[75];
(b) a body corporate controlled[76] by the trustees[77]; or
(c) a body corporate recognised under s 9 of the Administration of Justice Act 1985[78].

Section 19 further provides that trustees may appoint one of their number to act as nominee or custodian if that trustee is a trust corporation, or two or more of their number if they are to act as joint custodians or nominees[79]. A person who is appointed an agent, custodian or nominee may also be appointed to the other roles[80].

5.38 The power to appoint a custodian becomes a duty in certain circumstances. Trustees must appoint a custodian to hold bearer securities, unless:

---

68   Trustee Act 2000, s 16(2).
69   As defined by the Public Trustee Act 1906.
70   Trustee Act 2000, s 16(3).
71   Ibid, s 17(2).
72   Ibid, s 17(1).
73   Ibid, s 17(3).
74   Ibid, s 17(4).
75   Ibid, s 19(2)(a).
76   As defined by s 840 of the Income and Corporation Taxes Act 1988.
77   Trustee Act 2000, s 19(2)(b).
78   Ibid, s 19(2)(c).
79   Ibid, s 19(5).
80   Ibid, ss 19(6) and (7).

(a) the trustees are given power (by the trust deed or otherwise) to hold such investments themselves[81];

(b) there is a trust corporation acting as sole trustee[82];

(c) the trust has a custodian trustee[83]; or

(d) the assets in question are vested in the official custodian for charities[84].

This replaces s 7(1) of the 1925 Act, but permits a wider class than the 'banker or banking company' required by that section to act as custodian. Any appointment made under s 18 must be either made or evidenced in writing[85].

5.39 Section 20 makes provision for the remuneration and terms of appointment of custodians and nominees. As regards remuneration, the provisions of ss 29–32 are applied in the same way as for the appointment of agents. The reader is therefore referred to the discussion of these provisions at para **5.20**. Similarly, terms permitting the appointment of substitutes, restrictions of liability, and conflicts of interest may only be authorised if 'reasonably necessary'[86], echoing the provisions of s 14 in respect of agents[87].

THE DUTY TO REVIEW

5.40 Where trustees avail themselves of their new powers[88] and appoint an agent, custodian or nominee, they are under a duty to keep under review both the arrangements put in place, and how those arrangements are being carried out[89]. Having reviewed the situation, the trustees are under a duty to consider whether there is any necessity for them to use any of the powers of intervention[90] retained when appointing the agent, custodian or nominee[91]. If they do consider that there is a need to exercise any such powers, the trustees are under a duty to exercise them[92].

---

81   Trustee Act 2000, s 18(1).
82   Ibid, s 25(2).
83   Ibid, s 18(4).
84   Ibid, s 18(4).
85   Ibid, s 18(3).
86   Ibid, ss 20(2) and (3).
87   See paras **5.17** *et seq.*
88   The wording of s 21: '... where the trustees have, under section 11, 16, 17 or 18 ...' suggests that where trustees use powers under the trust instrument, the duty to review imposed by that section does not apply.
89   Section 22(1)(a).
90   The term 'Power of intervention' is defined by s 23(4) as including (and therefore not being limited to): (a) a power to give directions to the agent, custodian or nominee; and (b) a power to revoke the authorisation or appointment.
91   Section 22(1)(b).
92   Section 22(1)(c).

5.41 Section 22 therefore requires trustees to 'keep an eye' on the activities of their agents, custodians and nominees and to use the powers at their disposal to control them. The Act does not provide how regularly the trustees must carry out the reviews, but again, this is probably a question of fact for each case, as individual trusts will invariably require different levels of supervision.

5.42 Further and more specific, guidance is given as to the duty to review where trustees delegate their asset management functions to an agent. The duties under s 22(1) referred to in the previous paragraph are stated to include:

(a) a duty to consider whether there is any need to revise or replace the policy statement made in compliance with s 15[93];

(b) a duty to revise or replace the statement if they consider there to be a need to do so[94]; and

(c) a duty to assess whether the agent is complying with the statement currently in force[95].

Where the trustees intervene, and revise or replace the statement, they must comply with s 15(3) and (4), ensuring that the guidance is formulated with a view to ensuring that the asset management functions are exercised in the best interests of the trust, and the policy statement is made or evidenced in writing[96].

5.43 Failures by the trustees to carry out their duties of review under s 22 with 'reasonable care and skill' will give rise to a claim for breach of the statutory duty of care[97]. However, the position of trustees' failing to carry out the duties at all would not seem to be caught by the statutory duty of care[98], and beneficiaries would seem to be left with the remedy of bringing a claim under the so-called 'common law' duty of care, provided s 23 does not prevent such a claim being brought[99].

TRUSTEES' LIABILITY FOR THE DEFAULTS OF AGENTS, CUSTODIANS AND NOMINEES

5.44 The Act gives trustees a surprisingly wide exemption from liability for the acts or defaults of their agents, nominees or custodians[100]. From the

---

93   Section 22(2)(a).
94   Section 22(2)(b).
95   Section 22(2)(c).
96   Section 22(3).
97   Schedule 1, para 3(1)(e).
98   See para **2.22**.
99   See para **5.44**.
100   Section 23.

wording of s 23, it would seem that the only circumstances in which a beneficiary can seek redress from trustees for the default of an agent, custodian or nominee are where the trustees are in breach of the statutory duty of care when entering into the arrangements for the agent, custodian or nominee's appointment[101] or when carrying out the review duties under s 22[102]. Otherwise, the trustees are '... not liable for any act or default of the agent, custodian or nominee.'[103]. If a strict construction of s 23 is adopted, the consequences for beneficiaries are extremely serious: only failures by the trustees within the limited scope of the statutory duty of care will be actionable against the trustees[104]. Thus where, for example, the trustees fail to carry out a review at all, it would seem that they have absolutely no remedy against the trustees (the statutory duty of care applying only when trustees are 'carrying out' the review duties). The question of whether s 23 should be construed so as to have this effect will therefore be one of the most important ones for the courts to answer. The alternative construction is that a failure to comply with the s 22 duty is a default of the trustee distinct from that of the agent, custodian or nominee, and thus outside the scope of s 23.

5.45 If the strict construction outlined in the preceding paragraph is indeed the correct one, the result is surprising. Beneficiaries are left without redress against a defaulting trustee, and will be forced to pursue the agent, custodian or nominee in respect of any loss caused. It is for that reason that the authors conclude it is likely that the courts will favour the wider construction.

OTHER MATTERS

5.46 One of the most important provisions is contained in s 24. This section provides that where trustees fail to act within the limits of their powers conferred by the Act when appointing agents, custodians or nominees to act on behalf of the trust, the appointment itself will not be invalidated. Therefore, where trustees delegate their asset management functions to an agent and fail to make or evidence the appointment in writing[105], whilst they may be in breach of their duty of care, the appointment itself will be valid.

---

101 Section 23(1)(a).
102 Section 23(1)(b).
103 Section 23(1).
104 See paras **2.19** *et seq*.
105 As required by s 15.

5.47   The provisions relating to the use of agents custodians and nominees, whilst referring to 'trustees' applies equally to trusts which have a sole trustee[106].

5.48   Part IV of the Act does achieve its aims of enabling delegation of trustees' functions in a much wider range of circumstances. It should enable trustees to make full use of the services of investment managers and similar professionals, and thereby (hopefully) improve the financial position of the trusts which they administer. However, a balance must be struck between making administration easier for trustees, and protecting the interests of beneficiaries. Perhaps the greatest weakness in the Act as a whole is that the imposition of the duty of care and the new powers of delegation do not interact in a particularly satisfactory way.

DELEGATION CHECKLIST

5.49   In practical terms, the most important issue for trustees is how to delegate properly, so that they will not be held liable under the duties of care under statute or common law for losses caused to the trust by errors concerning delegation. Whilst specific guidance as to the delegation of asset management functions is given elsewhere in this book[107], the following points are of general application and should be considered whenever trustees delegate their functions or employ custodians or nominees.

– Is the function it is proposed to delegate a 'delegable function'?
– Is the person to whom the function is to be delegated someone to whom such delegation is permitted?
– What is an appropriate level of remuneration?
– Is it 'reasonably necessary' to permit the agent to appoint a substitute; restrict the agent's liability; permit the agent to act in situations where there is a conflict of interests?
– Has an appropriate policy statement been formulated where it is proposed to delegate asset management functions?
– Is a written agreement necessary?
– What powers of intervention need to be reserved?
– Are there bearer securities which must be held by a custodian by virtue of s 18?
– How often do reviews need to be undertaken?
– What procedures are in place to ensure that the reviews are carried out as intended?

---

106   Section 25(1).
107   See form M at Appendix III.

SUMMARY

5.50 There follows a summary of the provisions concerning agents, custodians and nominees.

(1) Trustees may authorise an agent to exercise any or all of their 'delegable functions'[108].

(2) The extent of a trustee's 'delegable functions' will depend upon whether the trust is a charitable or non-charitable trust[109].

(3) Anyone may be appointed to act as an agent except for a beneficiary[110].

(4) Even a beneficiary who is also a trustee is prohibited from acting as the trustees' agent[111].

(5) An agent is subject to any duties which are attached to the function delegated to him[112].

(6) Certain terms may not be included in an agent, custodian or nominee's terms of appointment unless their inclusion is considered to be 'reasonably necessary'[113].

(7) Where asset management functions are delegated, the appointment of the agent must be in writing and a policy statement must be prepared[114].

(8) Nominees and/or custodians may be appointed to hold any trust assets other than those of trusts having a custodian trustee or any assets vested in the official custodian for charities[115].

(9) In certain circumstances, some assets must be vested in custodians[116].

(10) Only certain classes of person (natural or legal) may be appointed as a nominee or custodian[117].

(11) A person may be appointed to more than one of the roles of agent, custodian and nominee[118].

(12) Trustees are under a duty to keep the activities of their agents, custodians and nominees under review[119].

---

108 See para **5.9**.
109 See para **5.10**.
110 See para **5.16**. This position is, however, different as regards delegation by the tenant for life under a strict settlement, as to which see para **5.8**.
111 See para **5.16**.
112 See para **5.26**.
113 See paras **5.17** *et seq*.
114 See para **5.25**.
115 See para **5.35**.
116 See para **5.38**.
117 See para **5.37**.
118 Ibid.
119 See para **5.40**.

(13) If trustees comply with the statutory duty of care (where applicable) they are not liable for the defaults of their agents, custodians or nominees[120].

(14) If trustees exceed their powers when appointing agents, custodians or nominees the appointment is not invalidated[121].

(15) The powers conferred apply to trusts created both before and after commencement of the Act, and are subject to any restriction or exclusion imposed by the trust instrument or any enactment or provision of subordinate legislation.

---

120   See para **5.44**.
121   See para **5.46**.

Chapter 6

REMUNERATION OF TRUSTEES

'He is well paid that is well satisfied ...'[1]

INTRODUCTION

6.1 Most trusts[2] and wills drafted in the last 100 years contain a charging clause enabling a professional trustee to charge for his time. Therefore, in some respects it might be considered that there was little need for any default provisions to be introduced by the Trustee Act 2000.

6.2 However, this fails to recognise that trusts do sometimes arise unexpectedly, or are imposed by law, as on an intestacy where there are minor beneficiaries. It also fails to recognise the problems of the home-made will, or statutory trusts arising on intestacy.

6.3 One of the major difficulties where there is no charging clause is in attracting a sufficiently expert trustee. With the new powers of delegation introduced by the Act, it might be thought that this is relatively unimportant, but if a professional trustee with the necessary expertise can be appointed to act, that might prove considerably cheaper than delegating to an agent who will of course require to be paid.

6.4 Interestingly, the Trust Law Committee recommended against the introduction of a default charging clause on the basis that settlors and testators ought to be made aware that the trustees would be able to charge (although how often testators actually bother to read through the standard charging clause or have it explained to them is perhaps open to question), that such a clause could be open to abuse, and that it would drive a coach and horses through the general principle that a trustee must not profit from the trusts. None of these concerns would appear to outweigh the benefit to a trust of being able to appoint a suitably qualified and competent trustee.

THE LAW BEFORE THE TRUSTEE ACT 2000

6.5 In general terms and subject to a number of well defined exceptions, it was the duty of a trustee to act gratuitously, and he had no right to charge for his time and trouble[3]. This was based upon the general principle that a

---

1   Shakespeare, *The Merchant of Venice*, Act IV, scene 1.
2   With the exception, perhaps, of charitable trusts.
3   *Robinson v Pett* (1734) 3 P Wms 249.

trustee must not gain any financial benefit from the trust property, nor make any secret remuneration[4].

6.6 The exceptions to this general rule were (and indeed remain) as follows.

– Where the settlement or will provides for a professional trustee to be remunerated; this will of course be the most commonly found circumstance in practice[5].

– Where the beneficiaries are all of full age and capacity and have entered into a legally binding agreement with the trustees that they should be remunerated for their services[6].

– Where the rule in *Cradock v Piper*[7] applies. This rather odd exception to the general rule applies to allow a solicitor trustee acting on his own behalf and on behalf of a co-trustee in an action or matter (therefore only court proceedings) to charge profit costs if his firm so acting has not increased the costs which his co-trustee would have incurred.

– Where the Public Trustee is acting, he is allowed to charge such fees as are fixed from time to time by the Treasury[8].

– Where a custodian trustee is acting, he may charge such fees as would be charged by the Public Trustee for acting as a custodian trustee[9].

– Where on the insolvency of a company an independent trustee of a pension scheme is appointed, he is entitled to reasonable fees and expenses in priority to all other claimants[10].

– Where the court appoints a trust corporation other than the Public Trustee, it is empowered to authorise such remuneration as it thinks fit[11].

– Where the court appoints a trustee under the Judicial Trustees Act 1896, it may also authorise remuneration[12].

– Where the court authorises the trustee to charge as part of its inherent jurisdiction to so. This jurisdiction is used sparingly[13], and involves performing a balancing act whereby the need to protect the beneficiaries is weighed against the benefit of the trust being well administered

---

4   As exemplified in *Boardman v Phipps* [1967] 2 AC 246.
5   See form F at Appendix III for a modern standard charging clause.
6   *Re Sherwood* (1840) 3 Beav 338. Any agreement (which can still be made after the coming into force of the Trustee Act 2000), ought to be made either by deed, or before the trustee accepts office, so that there is consideration for it.
7   (1850) 1 Mac & G 664.
8   Public Trustee Act 1906, s 9 as amended.
9   Public Trustee Act 1906, s 4.
10   Pensions Act 1995, s 20.
11   Trustee Act 1925, s 42.
12   Judicial Trustees Act 1896, s 1 (5); in an application for the appointment of a judicial trustee, or indeed for the appointment of a trust corporation there should be included an application for remuneration to be fixed.
13   *Re Worthington* [1954] 1 WLR 526; *Re Duke of Norfolk's Settlement* [1982] Ch 61.

by a properly remunerated trustee[14]. There have been a number of cases where the court has allowed a trustee or fiduciary remuneration in cases where he has committed an innocent breach of trust, and while he has not been allowed to keep the profits, has been paid for work done[15].

– Where the trust property is abroad and it is the local custom to allow remuneration[16].

6.7 Looking at these general exceptions is not simply of academic interest. The Trustee Act 2000 does not in any way repeal the law in this area, and indeed where there is an express charging clause in the settlement or will, the reforms are within a very narrow compass. The Act provides a mechanism whereby trustees can charge if none of the above exceptions applies, and will undoubtedly obviate the necessity for an application to the court in cases where there is no charging clause.

SOME SPECIFIC PROBLEMS

6.8 Even in a settlement or a will where there is an express charging clause, the general rule is that it must be construed strictly against the trustee or personal representative[17]. This means that where a clause entitled a trustee to make professional charges, even where he could charge for his time and trouble expended, that would extend only to work done in his capacity as a solicitor, and would exclude all time spent on trust business which a lay person could have undertaken[18]. Hence the reason why well drafted express charging clauses include words such as: 'including acts which a trustee could have done personally'. The Act does address this point.

6.9 A further difficulty, even in cases where there is an express charging clause, is that for many purposes, payments under such a clause are regarded as a gift. This causes particular problems in the area of wills and administration of estates. If a solicitor witnesses a will under which he is authorised to charge as a professional trustee, the benefit of the charging clause will be regarded as a gift to him and as a beneficiary witnessing the execution of the will, he will be precluded from taking it[19]. This is clearly anomalous.

---

14   *Re Duke of Norfolk's Settlement* [1982] Ch 61 at 79.
15   *Boardman v Phipps* [1967] 2 AC 46; *O'Sullivan v Management Agency and Music Limited* [1985] QB 428.
16   *Chambers v Goldwin* (1804) 9 Ves 254.
17   *Re Gee* [1948] Ch 284.
18   *Re Chalinder and Herrington* [1907] 1 Ch 58.
19   Section 15 of the Wills Act 1837, and see *Re Barber* (1886) 31 Ch D 665 and *Re Pooley* (1888) 40 Ch D 1. The rule has never applied where the attesting witness was the partner of the solicitor trustee in whose favour the charging clause was made, see *Re Bunting* [1947] 2 NZLR 219.

6.10   Similarly, for the purposes of marshalling assets in an estate to see how debts should be paid and which gifts should abate, charging clauses are treated as gifts rather than debts of the estate, which have to be discharged before the legacies are paid[20]. Consequently, a personal representative would rank behind all the other creditors of the estate in being paid. Again, this position seems nonsensical in a modern context, and the Act tackles both of these situations.

STRUCTURE OF THE ACT IN RELATION TO REMUNERATION

6.11   The new Act differentiates between:

–   the case where there is a professional charging clause in the trust or will[21];
–   trust corporations[22];
–   cases where there is no charging clause and the trustee is neither a trust corporation, a charitable trustee, nor a sole trustee[23];
–   charitable trusts[24];
–   agents, nominees and custodians[25].

WHERE THERE IS AN EXPRESS CHARGING CLAUSE

6.12   There is no distinction drawn between trustees of pension trusts and other trustees. During the consultation process there was overwhelming support for these new provisions relating to remuneration to apply to pensions fund trustees[26], and the new Act reflects that.

Application

6.13   The substantive provisions in s 28 apply to a trustee where there is:

'a provision in the trust instrument entitling him to receive payment out of trust funds in respect of services provided by him to or on behalf of the trust . . .'[27]

This appears wide enough to encompass all commonly found express charging clauses. The provisions, however, only apply 'except to the extent

---

20   Section 34(3) of the Administration of Estates Act 1925.
21   Dealt with by s 28.
22   Dealt with by s 29(1).
23   Dealt with by s 29(2) *et seq.*
24   Section 30.
25   Section 32.
26   Paragraph 7.20 of the Report.
27   Section 28(1)(a).

(if any) to which the trust instrument makes inconsistent provision'[28]. Therefore, if the trust instrument makes it clear that the solicitor is not to be remunerated for work which a lay trustee could perform, or that the remuneration he receives is to be treated as a gift, the provisions of s 28(2) and (4) would clearly not apply.

Services which a lay trustee could perform

6.14 A trustee is to be treated as entitled to remuneration under the trust instrument (unless, of course, its provisions are inconsistent with that) in respect of services even if they could have been performed by a lay trustee[29]. A lay trustee is defined as a trustee who is not a trust corporation and does not act in a professional capacity[30]. Although most well-drafted charging clauses provide that a solicitor trustee should be remunerated in such circumstances, this new provision will cover the situation where the charging clause is silent on the point. In such cases, the common law rule is that the clause must be construed against the trustee, and he will not be able to charge for business outside his profession as a solicitor[31].

6.15 This provision applies only to a trustee of a charitable trust who is not a trust corporation only if he is not a sole trustee[32] and to the extent that a majority of the trustees have agreed that it should apply to him[33]. Charitable trustees have always, contrary to the usual rule, been able to act by way of a majority and this provision reflects that. There has been concern expressed about a solicitor trustee of a charity being entitled to claim remuneration for work which a lay trustee could have carried out for obvious reasons. On the other hand, many charitable trusts are now very sophisticated organisations, and there may be considerable advantage in having a trustee who can be properly remunerated. The safeguard is that a majority of his fellow trustees must approve it.

6.16 The above provisions, whether in relation to ordinary or charitable trustees, do not have effect in relation to services provided to or on behalf of the trust before the commencement of the Act[34].

Remuneration as a gift

6.17 Any payments to which the trustee is entitled are to be treated as remuneration for the purposes of s 15 of the Wills Act 1837 and s 34(2) of the

---

28   Section 28(1).
29   Section 28(2).
30   Section 28(6), and for the meaning of 'professional capacity', see para **6.28** below.
31   See para **6.8** above.
32   A situation which would be rare with a charitable trust.
33   Section 28(3).
34   Section 33(1).

Administration of Estates Act 1925[35]. This deals with the somewhat odd position that if a solicitor trustee witnesses the execution of a will, any charging clause in his favour will be treated for these purposes as a gift to him and will be invalid.

6.18   It further provides that the trustee's remuneration will be regarded as a debt of an estate, rather than a gift which can abate. It must be remembered that both these provisions are subject to any inconsistent provision in the will in question[36], and therefore if the will requires that the remuneration be treated as a gift rather than a debt of the estate, the provisions of the Trustee Act 2000 will not apply.

6.19   The above provisions do not have any application where the death occurred before the commencement of s 28[37].

WHERE THERE IS NO PROVISION IN THE TRUST INSTRUMENT OR LEGISLATION FOR CHARGING

Application

6.20   Section 29 of the Act applies only where a trustee is not entitled to remuneration under the trust instrument or by any enactment[38] or provision of subordinate legislation[39]. Therefore, apart from the obvious case where there is a charging clause in the trust instrument, it will not apply, for example, to the Public Trustee[40], or a custodian appointed where the public trustee might have been appointed[41] or where there is an independent trustee of a pension scheme of an insolvent company[42]. The section does not apply in respect of services provided to or on behalf of the trust before the commencement of the Act, but applies whenever the trust was created[43].

Trust corporations

6.21   The position in relation to trust corporations is relatively straightforward. A trust corporation which is not a trustee of a charitable trust is entitled to receive reasonable remuneration[44] out of the trust funds for any

---

35   Section 28(4).
36   Section 28(1).
37   Section 33(2), in other words, to deaths prior to 1 February 2001.
38   For example, the Public Trustee Act 1906.
39   Section 29(5).
40   Entitled to charge under the Public Trustee Act 1906, as amended.
41   Public Trustee Act 1906, s 4.
42   Pensions Act 1995, s 20.
43   Section 33(1), and therefore will not apply to services provided prior to 1 February 2001.
44   Defined in s 29(3), and discussed below.

services that the trust corporation provides to or on behalf of the trust[45]. It will be entitled to remuneration for services which are capable of being performed by a lay trustee[46].

6.22 Trust corporation bears the same meaning in the Trustee Act 2000 as it did for the purposes of the 1925 Act[47]. It means:

'... the Public Trustee or a corporation either appointed by the Court in any particular case to be a trustee, or entitled by rules made under sub-section (3) of section 4 of the Public Trustee Act 1906 to act as a custodian trustee.'[48]

This definition was extended to cover the Treasury Solicitor, the Official Solicitor and certain other official persons and trustees of charitable, ecclesiastical and public trusts[49]. It is further provided that the company in question must be a company constituted under the law of an EU Member State, be empowered under its constitution to undertake trust business and have an issued share capital of £250,000[50], of which not less than £100,000 is paid up[51].

Other trustees

6.23 A trustee who is not a trust corporation, or a trustee of a charitable trust or a sole trustee but who acts in a professional capacity[52], is entitled to receive reasonable remuneration[53] out of the trust funds for any services he provides to or on behalf of the trust if each other trustee has agreed in writing[54] that he may be remunerated for the services[55]. As with remuneration under this section for trust corporations, if such an agreement is forthcoming, he will be entitled to remuneration even if the services in question are capable of being performed by a lay trustee[56].

6.24 A trustee who has been authorised under the powers of delegation contained in Part IV[57] of the Act to exercise any functions of the trustees as a whole or to act as a nominee or custodian is also entitled to remuneration under these provisions if all other conditions are fulfilled[58]. Therefore, for example if A and B who are lay trustees, delegate their investment powers to

---

45 Section 29(1).
46 Section 29(4).
47 Section 39(1).
48 Section 68(17) of the Trustee Act 1925.
49 Law of Property (Amendment) Act 1926, s 3 and Charities Act 1993, s 35.
50 Or its foreign currency equivalent.
51 Public Trustee (Custodian Trustee) Rules 1975, SI 1975/1189.
52 As defined in s 28(5) and as to which see para **6.28** below.
53 As defined in s 29(3) and as to which see para **6.25** below.
54 A precedent for such an agreement is form G at Appendix III.
55 Section 29(2).
56 Section 29(4).
57 As to which, see Chapter 5 above.
58 Section 29(6).

their co-trustee C who is a solicitor, C is able to charge for the services he provides to and on behalf of the trust including all the additional services he provides because of the functions which have been delegated to him by his co-trustees.

REASONABLE REMUNERATION

6.25 'Reasonable remuneration' means 'in relation to the provision of services by a trustee, such remuneration as is reasonable in the circumstances for the provision of those services to or on behalf of the trust by the trustee'[59]. It is unlikely that in practice there will be much difficulty about what is reasonable remuneration.

6.26 Specifically in relation to trust corporations, it is provided that such remuneration 'includes in relation to the provision of services by a trustee who is authorised under the Banking Act 1987 and provides services in that capacity, the institution's reasonable charges for the provision of such services'[60]. This is a particularly important provision (introduced by amendment at committee stage) for the bank trust companies who might otherwise have found it difficult to charge for their banking services, in circumstances where they would have had no problem charging if they were not the trustees of a particular trust or estate.

PROFESSIONAL CAPACITY

6.27 Throughout these provisions is the concept of the trustee acting in a 'professional capacity'. There was some concern expressed at consultation stage, that a professional wholly unconnected with the administration of trusts, who was a trustee, might be able to charge for his services and time. Therefore, a brain surgeon who was also a trustee would be able to charge for the time he spent administering the trust.

6.28 To ensure that this was not a problem, the Act provides[61] that a trustee acts in a professional capacity if he acts in the course of a profession or business which consists of or includes the provision of services in connection with the management or administration of trusts generally or a particular kind of trust[62], or any particular aspect of the management or adminis-

---

59   Section 29(3).
60   Ibid.
61   Section 28(5).
62   Section 28(5)(a).

tration of trusts generally or a particular kind of trust[63], and the services he provides to or on behalf of the trust fall within that description.

6.29   The section quite clearly does not confine the ability to charge to solicitors. In fact, it is doubtful whether a solicitor with a criminal or personal injury practice, who was appointed trustee of a family trust, but had no other experience in respect of the administration or management of trusts could be said to be acting in the course of a profession which consists of the provision of services in connection with the management or administration of trusts. Having said that, it is possible to construe the section in such a way that anyone who is a trustee and belongs to a profession which has people in it who provide services in respect of the administration and management of trusts, that will be sufficient. Certainly the section will apply to accountants, and stockbrokers who administer funds.

ADMINISTRATION OF ESTATES

6.30   It has already been noted that a charging clause is no longer regarded as a legacy for the purposes of determining the way in which assets are to be applied[64]. The Trustee Act 2000 further provides[65] that remuneration to which personal representatives are entitled under ss 28 and 29 of the Act, is to be treated as an administration expense for the purpose of s 34(3) of the Administration of Estates Act 1925[66] and for the purpose of Sch 6 to the Insolvency Act 1986[67].

6.31   These provisions do not apply in relation to any death occurring before this commencement of this section of the Act[68].

REMUNERATION OF TRUSTEES OF CHARITABLE TRUSTS

6.32   The proposal to include charitable trustees within the provisions to remunerate trustees where there is no charging clause in the charitable trust has been somewhat controversial, although it achieved considerable support during the consultation process[69]. The arguments in favour of having

---

63   Section 28(5)(b).
64   See para **6.17**.
65   Section 35(3).
66   Which governs the order in which an estate is to be paid out.
67   Which provides for administration expenses to have precedence over certain preferential debts listed there.
68   Section 35(4). In other words, before 1 February 2001.
69   See para 7.21 of the Report.

the power to remunerate trustees are that charities like other trusts need well qualified people to act as trustees, and being able to remunerate them could well be cheaper than employing agents to do so. Against this, however, is the fact that statutory default powers should reflect best drafting practice, and it is not the practice to include professional charging clauses as a matter of course in charitable trusts. Moreover, charitable trusts exist for public benefit and the volunteer ethos should therefore not be undermined. Many professionals do of course give their time freely to the charitable sector.

6.33 It was accordingly recognised that further consultation was required with the charity sector before any final provisions were put into place. It is therefore provided that the Secretary of State may by regulations make provisions for the remuneration of trustees of charitable trusts who are trust corporations or who act in a professional capacity[70]. The power includes the power to make provision for the remuneration of a trustee authorised by Part IV of the Act to exercise functions as an agent of the trustees or to act as an agent or nominee[71]. It therefore empowers the Secretary of State to make regulations allowing a trustee to charge for services where his co-trustees have delegated their powers to him, or have appointed him to act as a custodian or nominee.

6.34 The section further provides that regulations may make different provisions for different cases, and contain such supplemental, incidental, consequential and transitional provisions as the Secretary of State considers appropriate[72]. Significantly, the section provides for regulations to be made by statutory instrument, but only if a draft of it has been laid before Parliament and approved by a resolution of each House[73]. This recognises the importance with which any proposed reforms of this area are regarded.

TRUSTEES' EXPENSES

6.35 Trustees have always been entitled to be reimbursed out of the trust fund for expenses properly incurred by them[74]. That right operates as a first charge on the capital and income of the fund[75]. The Trustee Act 2000 confirms this position by providing that a trustee is entitled to be reimbursed

---

70   Section 30(1).
71   Section 30(2).
72   Section 30(3).
73   Section 30(4).
74   See, for a modern example, *Holding and Management Limited v Property Holding and Investment plc* [1990] 1 WLR 1313.
75   *X v A* [2000] 1 All ER 490.

from the trust funds, or may pay out of the trust funds[76] expenses properly incurred by him when acting on behalf of the trust[77]. It is therefore still necessary for the trustee to show that the expenses incurred by him were reasonable and proper in the circumstances[78].

6.36 The section applies to a trustee who has been authorised under Part IV of the Act to exercise the powers of a trustee or to act as a nominee or custodian as it applies to any other trustee[79]. Therefore, if trustees delegate their functions to one of their number, he is entitled to reimburse himself for any expenses incurred in exercising those delegated powers, as well as his ordinary role.

6.37 The Act does not apply to expenses incurred before the commencement of the Act[80], but applies to trusts whenever created[81].

REMUNERATION AND EXPENSES OF AGENTS, NOMINEES AND CUSTODIANS

6.38 Section 32 of the Act provides for the remuneration of agents, nominees and custodians and reimbursement of expenses incurred by them. The provisions do not apply only to agents, nominees and custodians appointed under Part IV of the Act, but cover those appointed under an express power contained in the trust instrument, or under any power conferred by the trustees by statute or subordinate legislation[82].

6.39 The provisions also apply to charitable trustees who have delegated their delegable functions under s 11(3) of the Act. This gives rise to the somewhat anomalous position that, at present, the charitable trustees cannot themselves be remunerated if there is no charging clause in the charitable trust, pending the making of regulations by the Secretary of State. This is also the position if trustees of a charitable trust delegate to one of their number. If, however, they delegate to a third party (which might prove to be a great deal more costly) they may remunerate him.

---

76 The first draft of the Bill did not include this provision, but a member of the Chancery Bar made the point that trustees usually paid sums out of the trust fund directly to defray expenses rather than reimbursing themselves.
77 Section 31(1).
78 *Malcolm v O'Callaghan* (1837) 3 May & Cr 52 where the costs of a trip to Paris by the trustee to see a court case in which the trust was involved were disallowed.
79 Section 31(2).
80 But these should be recoverable in most cases under the previous law.
81 Section 33(1).
82 Section 32(1).

6.40   The trustees may remunerate an agent, nominee or custodian if he is engaged on terms entitling him to be remunerated for those services[83], and the amount does not exceed such remuneration as is reasonable in the circumstances for the provision of those services by him to or on behalf of the trust[84]. It is most unlikely that agents, nominees or custodians will agree to act for trustees unless it is on terms that they are remunerated. From a practical point of view, it is important that trustees are fully aware before they delegate any of their functions or before they appoint a custodian or nominee, of the level of remuneration to be charged. It seems clear that they will be in breach of their statutory duty of care[85] if they agree remuneration with the agent which is not reasonable. The trustees should clearly shop around when looking for a suitable agent, nominee or custodian, in particular to get a feel for the sort of charges prevailing in the marketplace. It is not uncommon now for large trusts and, in particular, pension trusts to hold so-called 'beauty parades' for investment managers, to decide not only whether they will be the right agents for the job, but also to compare prices. From the point of view of the small trust, it is clearly important that the charges will be commensurate with its size.

6.41   The trustees may reimburse the agent, nominee or custodian out of the trust funds for any expenses properly incurred by him in exercising function as an agent, nominee or custodian[86]. This provision is clearly necessary, otherwise it could be argued that the expense was incurred by the agent, nominee or custodian, rather than by the trustee.

6.42   These provisions do not apply to services provided or expenses incurred on or before the commencement of the Act, but apply whenever the trust was created[87].

SUMMARY

6.43   There follows a summary of the provisions in relation to remuneration.

(1)   Where there is a charging clause in the trust instrument:
  –   trustees acting in a professional capacity can charge for services which a lay trustee could have performed[88];

---

83   Section 32(2)(a).
84   Section 32(2)(b). For a more detailed discussion of reasonable remuneration in the context of agents, custodians or nominees, see para **5.21** in Chapter 5 above.
85   Paragraph 3 of Sch 1 to the Act.
86   Section 32(3).
87   Section 33(1).
88   See para **6.17**.

- charitable trustees can charge for services which a lay trustee could have performed if not sole trustees and to the extent that a majority of co-trustees agree[89];
- payments under charging clauses in wills are no longer regarded as gifts[90].

(2) Where there is no charging clause in the trust instrument:
- trust corporations can charge reasonable remuneration[91];
- trustees acting in a professional capacity who are not sole trustees or charitable trustees can charge reasonable remuneration if each other trustee has agreed in writing[92];
- trustees acting in a professional capacity to whom co-trustees have delegated functions can charge reasonable remuneration if each other trustee has agreed in writing[93].

(3) The Secretary of State is empowered to make regulations regarding the remuneration of charitable trustees pending further consultation[94].

(4) Trustees can reimburse themselves or pay out of the trust fund expenses properly incurred by them[95].

(5) Agents, nominees and custodians may be remunerated and their expenses reimbursed[96].

(6) The provisions apply to trusts whenever created, but not to services provided or expenses incurred before the commencement of the Act[97].

---

89   See para **6.15**.
90   See para **6.17**.
91   See para **6.21**.
92   See para **6.23**.
93   See para **6.24**.
94   See para **6.32**.
95   See para **6.35**.
96   See para **6.38**.
97   See paras **6.19**, **6.31**, **6.37** and **6.42**.

Chapter 7

INSURANCE

'Adversity makes a man wise, not rich.'[1]

INTRODUCTION

7.1　Tucked away in the Miscellaneous and Supplementary section of the Act, is a significant reform of trustees' powers, which undoubtedly merits a chapter on its own. This is the reform of the trustees' powers to insure trust property, which is achieved by extensive amendment (if not in reality replacement) of s 19 of the Trustee Act 1925 (the 1925 Act).

7.2　A distinction has to be drawn between the power of trustees to insure trust property, and their duty to do so. The Act addresses the problems associated with trustees' powers, which under the previous law were an unsatisfactory patchwork of statutory provisions, with a few hints at common law that trustees had such powers. It is perhaps hardly surprising that one of the first provisions in administrative clauses contained in a well-drafted trust or will, is the power to insure. What the Act deliberately does not address is what duty the trustees have to insure, and this is in the authors' view to be regretted, as the law is wholly uncertain.

THE POWER TO INSURE: THE PREVIOUS LAW

7.3　Section 19 of the 1925 Act before the amendment by the new Act, but after the amendments made by the Trusts of Land and Appointment of Trustees Act 1996 (the 1996 Act) read:

> '(1) A trustee may insure any personal property against loss or damage to any amount, including the amount of any insurance already on foot, not exceeding three fourth parts of the full value of the property, and pay the premiums for such insurance out of the income thereof or out of any income of any other property subject to the same trusts without obtaining the consent of any person who may be entitled wholly or partly to such income.
>
> (2) This section does not apply to any personal property which a trustee is bound forthwith to convey absolutely to any beneficiary upon being requested to do so.'

Apart from the obvious observation that the section was not happily drafted, the following additional points can be made in relation to it.

1　Proverb.

–   Since the coming into force of the 1996 Act, the section had applied only to personalty; the 1996 Act made provisions in respect of trusts of land, and trustees of strict settlements ceased to have any power to insure.
–   While the section covered all risks, it is only to the extent of three-quarters of the value of the property, which seems inexplicable.
–   Premiums were only payable out of income.
–   The section did not apply when the trustees held trust property on a bare trust.

7.4   As far as trusts of land are concerned, trustees had all the powers of an absolute owner for the purpose of exercising their functions as trustees[2]. This clearly would include a power to insure the land if that were in the best interests of the trust. One side-effect of the 1996 Act mentioned above was that s 19 of the 1925 Act was confined to personal property[3]. This was fine as far as trusts of land were concerned because of the very wide powers conferred on the trustees[4]. However, unwittingly, trustees of strict settlements, previously able to rely on s 19 of the 1925 Act were now no longer able to do so.

7.5   There has always been a question mark over whether there is a power implied by the common law enabling trustees to insure trust property, in the absence of any express or statutory power. Certainly, some cases have suggested such an implied power[5]. However, the position seemed doubtful at best, and trustees faced with a life tenant, unhappy that premiums were being paid out of the income of the fund, might well decide that failing to insure the trust property was the line of least resistance.

THE POWER TO INSURE

7.6   For s 19 of the 1925 Act is substituted a new section[6], which provides that a trustee may insure any property which is subject to the trust against risks of loss and damage due to any event[7] and pay the premiums out of the trust funds[8]. Trust funds are defined as 'any income or capital funds of the trust'[9]. This means that the trustee can decide whether to pay insurance premiums out of income or capital. This may be very important in a case

---

2   Section 6(1) of the 1996 Act.
3   Consequential amendments in Sch 3 to the 1996 Act.
4   Section 6(1) of the 1996 Act.
5   *Re Betty* [1899] 1 Ch 821 at 829.
6   By s 34 of the Trustee Act 2000.
7   Section 19(1)(a) of the Trustee Act 1925.
8   Ibid, s 19(1)(b).
9   Ibid, s 19(5).

where there is little income produced by the trust, but a capital fund is available.

7.7 Section 19 in its previous form, did not apply to bare trusts. It was considered by the Law Commission[10] that trustees of a bare trust ought to have the powers to insure conferred by the new Act, but subject to the beneficiaries being able to take those powers away. It is therefore provided that in the case of property held on a bare trust, the power to insure is subject to any direction given by the beneficiary[11] or each of the beneficiaries[12] that any property specified in the direction is not to be insured[13] and/or that any property specified in the direction is not to be insured except on such conditions as may be so specified[14]. Property is held on a bare trust if it is held on trust for a beneficiary of full age and capacity and absolutely entitled to the property subject to the trust[15], or for beneficiaries each of whom is of full age and capacity and who taken together are absolutely entitled to the property subject to the trust[16]. The latter situation envisages a trust where the beneficiaries could if they wished act together and put an end to the trust in accordance with the principles in *Saunders v Vautier*[17]. It clearly makes sense that in such a case the beneficiaries should be able to decide that trust monies should not be spent on insuring the assets of the trust. It does, however, rely on agreement between the beneficiaries that the power to insure should not apply, or should be restricted in some way. If such a direction is given by a beneficiary or beneficiaries, insofar as it restricts or excludes the power to insure, that ceases to be a delegable function for the purposes of s 11 of the new Act[18].

7.8 The amendments made to s 19 of the 1925 Act apply in relation to trusts whether created before or after the commencement of the new Act[19]. The new Act therefore confers on trustees of all types of trust, whether of land, or personalty, whether a trust of land under the 1996 Act, or still governed by the Settled Land Act 1925, wide powers to insure trust assets against all risks, and to pay the premiums for insuring out of the capital or income of the trust funds. When exercising this new power, trustees are subject to the statutory duty of care[20]. This does not mean that the trustees

---

10 Paragraph 6.5 of the Report.
11 In the case of a bare trust where there is only one person absolutely entitled.
12 In the case of a bare trust where all the beneficiaries are of full age and capacity and together are absolutely entitled as against the trustees.
13 Trustee Act 1925, s 19(2)(a).
14 Ibid, s 19(2)(b).
15 Ibid, s 19(3)(a).
16 Ibid, s 19(3)(b).
17 (1841) 4 Beav 115.
18 As to which see Chapter 5 above.
19 Section 34(3) of the Trustee Act 2000.
20 Ibid, Sch 1, para 4.

have imposed upon them a duty to insure. It is clear that they do not, and this was a deliberate decision on the part of the Law Commission in drafting the Bill. However, having decided that they wish to exercise their power to insure, the trustees are subject to the statutory duty of care. Therefore they must take care that the trust property is insured for its full value, and against sensible risks.

7.9 The statutory duty of care also applies to a power to insure however conferred[21]. Therefore, even if the trustees do not have to rely on the new powers contained in the amended s 19 of the 1925 Act, because they have the benefit of an express power, they must still take care in exercising that power, unless the trust instrument excludes the statutory duty of care[22].

THE DUTY TO INSURE

7.10 The Consultation Document recommended that trustees should be under a duty to insure trust property in circumstances when, against such risks as and for such amount as a reasonable prudent person would have insured the property[23]. Such a proposal was roundly rejected during the consultation process[24], concern being expressed that trustees might feel obliged to insure when it was unnecessary, or small trusts might simply lack the resources to insure.

7.11 The difficulty in any duty to insure being omitted from the Trustee Act 2000, is that the common law position is by no means clear. There is authority to the effect that trustees ought to insure the trust property[25]. On the other hand, there are some cases which have suggested that the trustees will not be liable for willful default (in effect breach of duty) if they fail to insure[26]. Those latter cases have been relied upon for the principle that even where there is a power to insure, a trustee will not be held liable for losses to the trust property occasioned by the failure to insure[27].

7.12 It is hard to reconcile this principle with the rule that a trustee must manage the trust estate with those precautions which an ordinary prudent man of business would take in managing similar affairs of his own[28]. The failure on the part of an ordinary man of business to keep his residence

---

21   Trustee Act 2000, Sch 1, para 4..
22   Which it can do under para 5 of Sch 1 to the Trustee Act 2000.
23   Paragraph 9.21 of the Consultation Document.
24   Paragraph 6.8 of the Report.
25   *Re Betty* [1899] 1 Ch 821 at 829.
26   *Bailey v Gould* (1840) 4 Y&C Ex 221 and *Fry v Fry* (1859) 28 LJ Ch 593.
27   *Re McEacharn* (1911) 103 LT 900.
28   *Bartlett v Barclays Bank Trust Co Ltd* [1980] Ch 515.

insured against the usual risks would hardly be regarded as prudent behaviour on his part. It is therefore difficult to see why as a trustee he would escape liability if he failed to keep a house, which formed part of the trust fund insured. It is not enough to say that with the introduction of the new wider statutory power there will be no excuse if the trustees do not insure. If one of the trustees refused to exercise the power to insure the trust property, the court would have no jurisdiction to interfere with this exercise of discretion. On the other hand, if the trustees were under a duty to insure, the court could clearly intervene and order them to do so.

7.13 It is the authors' view that if trustees now failed to insure trust property which the ordinary prudent man of business would insure if it were his own, they will be held liable for any loss caused to the trust fund. In other words, the old authorities which suggest that a trustee will not be guilty of willful default for failing to insure would not be followed if the matter came before the courts today.

7.14 Therefore, notwithstanding the fact that no duty to insure is imposed by the Act, trustees cannot assume that they are safe from attack on the basis that they have failed to insure when they should have done. The better view is almost certainly that in deciding whether or not to exercise the new statutory power to insure, they should take such care as the ordinary prudent man of business would do in managing his own affairs. Having decided to exercise the statutory power, they will be subject to the statutory duty of care.

SUMMARY

7.15 There follows a summary of the provisions relating to insurance.

(1) Trustees have the power to insure trust property and pay for premiums out of the capital or income of the trust fund[29].
(2) In respect of bare trusts, the power is subject to the direction of the beneficiary or each of the beneficiaries as to whether assets should be insured and/or on what terms[30].
(3) The exercise of the new statutory power (and any other power to insure) is subject to the statutory duty of care[31].
(4) The provisions apply to trusts whenever created.

---

29   See para **7.6**.
30   See para **7.7**.
31   See para **7.8**.

Appendix I

TRUSTEE ACT 2000

(2000 c 29)

ARRANGEMENT OF SECTIONS

PART I

THE DUTY OF CARE

Section		Page
1	The duty of care	111
2	Application of duty of care	111

PART II

INVESTMENT

3	General power of investment	111
4	Standard investment criteria	112
5	Advice	112
6	Restriction or exclusion of this Part etc	112
7	Existing trusts	113

PART III

ACQUISITION OF LAND

8	Power to acquire freehold and leasehold land	113
9	Restriction or exclusion of this Part etc	113
10	Existing trusts	114

PART IV

AGENTS, NOMINEES AND CUSTODIANS

Agents

11	Power to employ agents	114
12	Persons who may act as agents	115
13	Linked functions etc	115
14	Terms of agency	115
15	Asset management: special restrictions	116

Nominees and custodians

16	Power to appoint nominees	116
17	Power to appoint custodians	117
18	Investment in bearer securities	117
19	Persons who may be appointed as nominees or custodians	117
20	Terms of appointment of nominees and custodians	118

Review of and liability for agents, nominees and custodians etc

21	Application of sections 22 and 23	118
22	Review of agents, nominees and custodians etc	119
23	Liability for agents, nominees and custodians etc	119

Supplementary

24	Effect of trustees exceeding their powers	120
25	Sole trustees	120
26	Restriction or exclusion of this Part etc	120
27	Existing trusts	120

PART V

REMUNERATION

28	Trustee's entitlement to payment under trust instrument	120
29	Remuneration of certain trustees	121
30	Remuneration of trustees of charitable trusts	122
31	Trustees' expenses	122
32	Remuneration and expenses of agents, nominees and custodians	123
33	Application	123

PART VI

MISCELLANEOUS AND SUPPLEMENTARY

34	Power to insure	123
35	Personal representatives	124
36	Pension schemes	125
37	Authorised unit trusts	126
38	Common investment schemes for charities etc	126
39	Interpretation	126
40	Minor and consequential amendments etc	127
41	Power to amend other Acts	127
42	Commencement and extent	127
43	Short title	127

SCHEDULES:

Schedule 1 – Application of duty of care 128
Schedule 2 – Minor and consequential amendments 129
    Part I – The Trustee Investments Act 1961 and the Charities Act
      1993 129
    Part II – Other Public General Acts 130
    Part III – Measures 138
Schedule 3 – Transitional provisions and savings 140
Schedule 4 – Repeals 142
    Part I – The Trustee Investments Act 1961 and the Charities Act
      1993 142
    Part II – Other repeals 142

An Act to amend the law relating to trustees and persons having the investment powers of trustees; and for connected purposes. [23 November 2000]

PART I

THE DUTY OF CARE

1 The duty of care

(1) Whenever the duty under this subsection applies to a trustee, he must exercise such care and skill as is reasonable in the circumstances, having regard in particular –

  (a) to any special knowledge or experience that he has or holds himself out as having, and
  (b) if he acts as trustee in the course of a business or profession, to any special knowledge or experience that it is reasonable to expect of a person acting in the course of that kind of business or profession.

(2) In this Act the duty under subsection (1) is called 'the duty of care'.

2 Application of duty of care

Schedule 1 makes provision about when the duty of care applies to a trustee.

PART II

INVESTMENT

3 General power of investment

(1) Subject to the provisions of this Part, a trustee may make any kind of investment that he could make if he were absolutely entitled to the assets of the trust.

(2) In this Act the power under subsection (1) is called 'the general power of investment'.

(3) The general power of investment does not permit a trustee to make investments in land other than in loans secured on land (but see also section 8).

(4) A person invests in a loan secured on land if he has rights under any contract under which –

(a) one person provides another with credit, and
(b) the obligation of the borrower to repay is secured on land.

(5) 'Credit' includes any cash loan or other financial accommodation.

(6) 'Cash' includes money in any form.

4 Standard investment criteria

(1) In exercising any power of investment, whether arising under this Part or otherwise, a trustee must have regard to the standard investment criteria.

(2) A trustee must from time to time review the investments of the trust and consider whether, having regard to the standard investment criteria, they should be varied.

(3) The standard investment criteria, in relation to a trust, are –

(a) the suitability to the trust of investments of the same kind as any particular investment proposed to be made or retained and of that particular investment as an investment of that kind, and
(b) the need for diversification of investments of the trust, in so far as is appropriate to the circumstances of the trust.

5 Advice

(1) Before exercising any power of investment, whether arising under this Part or otherwise, a trustee must (unless the exception applies) obtain and consider proper advice about the way in which, having regard to the standard investment criteria, the power should be exercised.

(2) When reviewing the investments of the trust, a trustee must (unless the exception applies) obtain and consider proper advice about whether, having regard to the standard investment criteria, the investments should be varied.

(3) The exception is that a trustee need not obtain such advice if he reasonably concludes that in all the circumstances it is unnecessary or inappropriate to do so.

(4) Proper advice is the advice of a person who is reasonably believed by the trustee to be qualified to give it by his ability in and practical experience of financial and other matters relating to the proposed investment.

6 Restriction or exclusion of this Part etc

(1) The general power of investment is –

(a) in addition to powers conferred on trustees otherwise than by this Act, but
(b) subject to any restriction or exclusion imposed by the trust instrument or by any enactment or any provision of subordinate legislation.

(2) For the purposes of this Act, an enactment or a provision of subordinate legislation is not be regarded as being, or as being part of, a trust instrument.

(3) In this Act 'subordinate legislation' has the same meaning as in the Interpretation Act 1978.

7   Existing trusts

(1) This Part applies in relation to trusts whether created before or after its commencement.

(2) No provision relating to the powers of a trustee contained in a trust instrument made before 3 August 1961 is to be treated (for the purposes of section 6(1)(b)) as restricting or excluding the general power of investment.

(3) A provision contained in a trust instrument made before the commencement of this Part which –

   (a)   has effect under section 3(2) of the Trustee Investments Act 1961 as a power to invest under that Act, or
   (b)   confers power to invest under that Act,

is to be treated as conferring the general power of investment on a trustee.

PART III

ACQUISITION OF LAND

8   Power to acquire freehold and leasehold land

(1) A trustee may acquire freehold or leasehold land in the United Kingdom –

   (a)   as an investment,
   (b)   for occupation by a beneficiary, or
   (c)   for any other reason.

(2) 'Freehold or leasehold land' means –

   (a)   in relation to England and Wales, a legal estate in land,
   (b)   in relation to Scotland –
      (i)   the estate or interest of the proprietor of the dominium utile or, in the case of land not held on feudal tenure, the estate or interest of the owner, or
      (ii)   a tenancy, and
   (c)   in relation to Northern Ireland, a legal estate in land, including land held under a fee farm grant.

(3) For the purpose of exercising his functions as a trustee, a trustee who acquires land under this section has all the powers of an absolute owner in relation to the land.

9   Restriction or exclusion of this Part etc

The powers conferred by this Part are –

   (a)   in addition to powers conferred on trustees otherwise than by this Part, but

(b)   subject to any restriction or exclusion imposed by the trust instrument or by any enactment or any provision of subordinate legislation.

10   Existing trusts

(1) This Part does not apply in relation to –

(a)   a trust of property which consists of or includes land which (despite section 2 of the Trusts of Land and Appointment of Trustees Act 1996) is settled land, or
(b)   a trust to which the Universities and College Estates Act 1925 applies.

(2) Subject to subsection (1), this Part applies in relation to trusts whether created before or after its commencement.

PART IV

AGENTS, NOMINEES AND CUSTODIANS

Agents

11   Power to employ agents

(1) Subject to the provisions of this Part, the trustees of a trust may authorise any person to exercise any or all of their delegable functions as their agent.

(2) In the case of a trust other than a charitable trust, the trustees' delegable functions consist of any function other than –

(a)   any functions relating to whether or in what way any assets of the trust should be distributed,
(b)   any power to decide whether any fees or other payment due to be made out of the trust funds should be made out of income or capital,
(c)   any power to appoint a person to be a trustee of the trust, or
(d)   any power conferred by any other enactment or the trust instrument which permits the trustees to delegate any of their functions or to appoint a person to act as a nominee or custodian.

(3) In the case of a charitable trust, the trustees' functions are –

(a)   any function consisting of carrying out a decision that the trustees have taken;
(b)   any function relating to the investment of assets subject to the trust (including, in the case of land held as an investment, managing the land and creating or disposing of an interest in the land);
(c)   any function relating to the raising of funds for the trust otherwise than by means of profits of a trade which is an integral part of carrying out the trust's charitable purpose;
(d)   any other function prescribed by an order made by the Secretary of State.

(4) For the purposes of subsection (3)(c) a trade is an integral part of carrying out a trust's charitable purpose if, whether carried on in the United Kingdom or elsewhere, the profits are applied solely to the purposes of the trust and either –

(a) the trade is exercised in the course of the actual carrying out of a primary purpose of the trust, or

(b) the work in connection with the trade is mainly carried out by beneficiaries of the trust.

(5) The power to make an order under subsection (3)(d) is exercisable by statutory instrument which shall be subject to annulment in pursuance of a resolution of either House of Parliament.

12 Persons who may act as agents

(1) Subject to subsection (2), the persons whom the trustees may under section 11 authorise to exercise functions as their agent include one or more of their number.

(2) The trustees may not authorise two (or more) persons to exercise the same function unless they are to exercise the function jointly.

(3) The trustees may not under section 11 authorise a beneficiary to exercise any function as their agent (even if the beneficiary is also a trustee).

(4) The trustees may under section 11 authorise a person to exercise functions as their agent even though he is also appointed to act as their nominee or custodian (whether under section 16, 17 or 18 or any other power).

13 Linked functions etc

(1) Subject to subsections (2) and (5), a person who is authorised under section 11 to exercise a function is (whatever the terms of the agency) subject to any specific duties or restrictions attached to the function.

For example, a person who is authorised under section 11 to exercise the general power of investment is subject to the duties under section 4 in relation to that power.

(2) A person who is authorised under section 11 to exercise a power which is subject to a requirement to obtain advice is not subject to the requirement if he is the kind of person from whom it would have been proper for the trustees, in compliance with the requirement, to obtain advice.

(3) Subsections (4) and (5) apply to a trust to which section 11(1) of the Trusts of Land and Appointment of Trustees Act 1996 (duties to consult beneficiaries and give effect to their wishes) applies.

(4) The trustees may not under section 11 authorise a person to exercise any of their functions on terms that prevent them from complying with section 11(1) of the 1996 Act.

(5) A person who is authorised under section 11 to exercise any function relating to land subject to the trust is not subject to section 11(1) of the 1996 Act.

14 Terms of agency

(1) Subject to subsection (2) and sections 15(2) and 29 to 32, the trustees may authorise a person to exercise functions as their agent on such terms as to remuneration and other matters as they may determine.

(2) The trustees may not authorise a person to exercise functions as their agent on any of the terms mentioned in subsection (3) unless it is reasonably necessary for them to do so.

(3) The terms are –

  (a) a term permitting the agent to appoint a substitute;
  (b) a term restricting the liability of the agent or his substitute to the trustees or any beneficiary;
  (c) a term permitting the agent to act in circumstances capable of giving rise to a conflict of interest.

15 Asset management: special restrictions

(1) The trustees may not authorise a person to exercise any of their asset management functions as their agent except by an agreement which is in or evidenced in writing.

(2) The trustees may not authorise a person to exercise any of their asset management functions as their agent unless –

  (a) they have prepared a statement that gives guidance as to how the functions should be exercised ('a policy statement'), and
  (b) the agreement under which the agent is to act includes a term to the effect that he will secure compliance with –
    (i)   the policy statement, or
    (ii) if the policy statement is revised or replaced under section 22, the revised or replacement policy statement.

(3) The trustees must formulate any guidance given in the policy statement with a view to ensuring that the functions will be exercised in the best interests of the trust.

(4) The policy statement must be in or evidenced in writing.

(5) The asset management functions of trustees are their functions relating to –

  (a) the investment of assets subject to the trust,
  (b) the acquisition of property which is to be subject to the trust, and
  (c) managing property which is subject to the trust and disposing of, or creating or disposing of an interest in, such property.

Nominees and custodians

16 Power to appoint nominees

(1) Subject to the provisions of this Part, the trustees of a trust may –

  (a) appoint a person to act as their nominee in relation to such of the assets of the trust as they determine (other than settled land), and
  (b) take such steps as are necessary to secure that those assets are vested in a person so appointed.

(2) An appointment under this section must be in or evidenced in writing.

(3) This section does not apply to any trust having a custodian trustee or in relation to any assets vested in the official custodian for charities.

17 Power to appoint custodians

(1) Subject to the provisions of this Part, the trustees of a trust may appoint a person to act as a custodian in relation to such of the assets of the trust as they may determine.

(2) For the purposes of this Act a person is a custodian in relation to assets if he undertakes the safe custody of the assets or of any documents or records concerning the assets.

(3) An appointment under this section must be in or evidenced in writing.

(4) This section does not apply to any trust having a custodian trustee or in relation to any assets vested in the official custodian for charities.

18 Investment in bearer securities

(1) If trustees retain or invest in securities payable to bearer, they must appoint a person to act as a custodian of the securities.

(2) Subsection (1) does not apply if the trust instrument or any enactment or provision of subordinate legislation contains provision which (however expressed) permits the trustees to retain or invest in securities payable to bearer without appointing a person to act as a custodian.

(3) An appointment under this section must be in or evidenced in writing.

(4) This section does not apply to any trust having a custodian trustee or in relation to any securities vested in the official custodian for charities.

19 Persons who may be appointed as nominees or custodians

(1) A person may not be appointed under section 16, 17 or 18 as a nominee or custodian unless one of the relevant conditions is satisfied.

(2) The relevant conditions are that –

  (a) the person carries on a business which consists of or includes acting as a nominee or custodian;
  (b) the person is a body corporate which is controlled by the trustees;
  (c) the person is a body corporate recognised under section 9 of the Administration of Justice Act 1985.

(3) The question whether a body corporate is controlled by trustees is to be determined in accordance with section 840 of the Income and Corporation Taxes Act 1988.

(4) The trustees of a charitable trust which is not an exempt charity must act in accordance with any guidance given by the Charity Commissioners concerning the selection of a person for appointment as a nominee or custodian under section 16, 17 or 18.

(5) Subject to subsections (1) and (4), the persons whom the trustees may under section 16, 17 or 18 appoint as a nominee or custodian include –

  (a) one of their number, if that one is a trust corporation, or
  (b) two (or more) of their number, if they are to act as joint nominees or joint custodians.

(6) The trustees may under section 16 appoint a person to act as their nominee even though he is also –

  (a) appointed to act as their custodian (whether under section 17 or 18 or any other power), or
  (b) authorised to exercise functions as their agent (whether under section 11 or any other power).

(7) Likewise, the trustees may under section 17 or 18 appoint a person to act as their custodian even though he is also –

  (a) appointed to act as their nominee (whether under section 16 or any other power), or
  (b) authorised to exercise functions as their agent (whether under section 11 or any other power).

20   Terms of appointment of nominees and custodians

(1) Subject to subsection (2) and sections 29 to 32, the trustees may under section 16, 17 or 18 appoint a person to act as a nominee or custodian on such terms as to remuneration and other matters as they may determine.

(2) The trustees may not under section 16, 17 or 18 appoint a person to act as a nominee or custodian on any of the terms mentioned in subsection (3) unless it is reasonably necessary for them to do so.

(3) The terms are –

  (a) a term permitting the nominee or custodian to appoint a substitute;
  (b) a term restricting the liability of the nominee or custodian or his substitute to the trustees or to any beneficiary;
  (c) a term permitting the nominee or custodian to act in circumstances capable of giving rise to a conflict of interest.

Review of and liability for agents, nominees and custodians etc

21   Application of sections 22 and 23

(1) Sections 22 and 23 apply in a case where trustees have, under section 11, 16, 17 or 18 –

  (a) authorised a person to exercise functions as their agent, or
  (b) appointed a person to act as a nominee or custodian.

(2) Subject to subsection (3), sections 22 and 23 also apply in a case where trustees have, under any power conferred on them by the trust instrument or by any enactment or any provision of subordinate legislation –

(a) authorised a person to exercise functions as their agent, or

(b) appointed a person to act as a nominee or custodian.

(3) If the application of section 22 or 23 is inconsistent with the terms of the trust instrument or the enactment or provision of subordinate legislation, the section in question does not apply.

22 Review of agents, nominees and custodians etc

(1) While the agent, nominee or custodian continues to act for the trust, the trustees –

(a) must keep under review the arrangements under which the agent, nominee or custodian acts and how those arrangements are being put into effect,

(b) if circumstances make it appropriate to do so, must consider whether there is a need to exercise any power of intervention that they have, and

(c) if they consider that there is a need to exercise such a power, must do so.

(2) If the agent has been authorised to exercise asset management functions, the duty under subsection (1) includes, in particular –

(a) a duty to consider whether there is any need to revise or replace the policy statement made for the purposes of section 15,

(b) if they consider that there is a need to revise or replace the policy statement, a duty to do so, and

(c) a duty to assess whether the policy statement (as it has effect for the time being) is being complied with.

(3) Subsections (3) and (4) of section 15 apply to the revision or replacement of a policy statement under this section as they apply to the making of a policy statement under that section.

(4) 'Power of intervention' includes –

(a) a power to give directions to the agent, nominee or custodian;

(b) a power to revoke the authorisation or appointment.

23 Liability for agents, nominees and custodians etc

(1) A trustee is not liable for any act or default of the agent, nominee or custodian unless he has failed to comply with the duty of care applicable to him, under paragraph 3 of Schedule 1 –

(a) when entering into the arrangements under which the person acts as agent, nominee or custodian, or

(b) when carrying out his duties under section 22.

(2) If a trustee has agreed a term under which the agent, nominee or custodian is permitted to appoint a substitute, the trustee is not liable for any act or default of the substitute unless he has failed to comply with the duty of care applicable to him, under paragraph 3 of Schedule 1 –

(a) when agreeing that term, or

(b) when carrying out his duties under section 22 in so far as they relate to the use of the substitute.

Supplementary

24   Effect of trustees exceeding their powers

A failure by the trustees to act within the limits of the powers conferred by this Part –

(a) in authorising a person to exercise a function of theirs as an agent, or

(b) in appointing a person to act as a nominee or custodian,

does not invalidate the authorisation or appointment.

25   Sole trustees

(1) Subject to subsection (2), this Part applies in relation to a trust having a sole trustee as it applies in relation to other trusts (and references in this Part to trustees – except in sections 12(1) and (3) and 19(5) – are to be read accordingly).

(2) Section 18 does not impose a duty on a sole trustee if that trustee is a trust corporation.

26   Restriction or exclusion of this Part etc

The powers conferred by this Part are –

(a) in addition to powers conferred on trustees otherwise than by this Act, but

(b) subject to any restriction or exclusion imposed by the trust instrument or by any enactment or any provision of subordinate legislation.

27   Existing trusts

This Part applies in relation to trusts whether created before or after its commencement.

PART V

REMUNERATION

28   Trustee's entitlement to payment under trust instrument

(1) Except to the extent (if any) to which the trust instrument makes inconsistent provision, subsections (2) to (4) apply to a trustee if –

(a) there is a provision in the trust instrument entitling him to receive payment out of trust funds in respect of services provided by him to or on behalf of the trust, and

(b) the trustee is a trust corporation or is acting in a professional capacity.

(2) The trustee is to be treated as entitled under the trust instrument to receive payment in respect of services even if they are services which are capable of being provided by a lay trustee.

(3) Subsection (2) applies to a trustee of a charitable trust who is not a trust corporation only –

    (a) if he is not a sole trustee, and

    (b) to the extent that a majority of the other trustees have agreed that it should apply to him.

(4) Any payments to which the trustee is entitled in respect of services are to be treated as remuneration for services (and not as a gift) for the purposes of –

    (a) section 15 of the Wills Act 1837 (gifts to an attesting witness to be void), and

    (b) section 34(3) of the Administration of Estates Act 1925 (order in which estate to be paid out).

(5) For the purposes of this Part, a trustee acts in a professional capacity if he acts in the course of a profession or business which consists of or includes the provision of services in connection with –

    (a) the management or administration of trusts generally or a particular kind of trust, or

    (b) any particular aspect of the management or administration of trusts generally or a particular kind of trust,

and the services he provides to or on behalf of the trust fall within that description.

(6) For the purposes of this Part, a person acts as a lay trustee if he –

    (a) is not a trust corporation, and

    (b) does not act in a professional capacity.

29   Remuneration of certain trustees

(1) Subject to subsection (5), a trustee who –

    (a) is a trust corporation, but

    (b) is not a trustee of a charitable trust,

is entitled to receive reasonable remuneration out of the trust funds for any services that the trust corporation provides to or on behalf of the trust.

(2) Subject to subsection (5), a trustee who –

    (a) acts in a professional capacity, but

    (b) is not a trust corporation, a trustee of a charitable trust or a sole trustee,

is entitled to receive reasonable remuneration out of the trust funds for any services that he provides to or on behalf of the trust if each other trusteee has agreed in writing that he may be remunerated for the services.

(3) 'Reasonable remuneration' means, in relation to the provision of services by a trustee, such remuneration as is reasonable in the circumstances for the provision of

those services to or on behalf of that trust by that trustee and for the purposes of subsection (1) includes, in relation to the provision of services by a trustee who is an authorised institution under the Banking Act 1987 and provides the services in that capacity, the institution's reasonable charges for the provision of such services.

(4) A trustee is entitled to remuneration under this section even if the services in question are capable of being provided by a lay trustee.

(5) A trustee is not entitled to remuneration under this section if any provision about his entitlement to remuneration has been made –

    (a) by the trust instrument, or
    (b) by any enactment or any provision of subordinate legislation.

(6) This section applies to a trustee who has been authorised under a power conferred by Part IV or the trust instrument –

    (a) to exercise functions as an agent of the trustees, or
    (b) to act as a nominee or custodian,

as it applies to any other trustee.

30   Remuneration of trustees of charitable trusts

(1) The Secretary of State may by regulations make provision for the remuneration of trustees of charitable trusts who are trust corporations or act in a professional capacity.

(2) The power under subsection (1) includes a power to make provision for the remuneration of a trustee who has been authorised under a power conferred by Part IV or any other enactment or any provision of subordinate legislation, or by the trust instrument –

    (a) to exercise functions as an agent of the trustees, or
    (b) to act as a nominee or custodian.

(3) Regulations under this section may –

    (a) make different provision for different cases;
    (b) contain such supplemental, incidental, consequential and transitional provision as the Secretary of State considers appropriate.

(4) The power to make regulations under this section is exercisable by statutory instrument, but no such instrument shall be made unless a draft of it has been laid before Parliament and approved by a resolution of each House of Parliament.

31   Trustees' expenses

(1) A trustee –

    (a) is entitled to be reimbursed from the trust funds, or
    (b) may pay out of the trust funds,

expenses properly incurred by him when acting on behalf of the trust.

(2) This section applies to a trustee who has been authorised under a power conferred by Part IV or any other enactment or any provision of subordinate legislation, or by the trust instrument –

(a) to exercise functions as an agent of the trustees, or
(b) to act as a nominee or custodian,

as it applies to any other trustee.

32 Remuneration and expenses of agents, nominees and custodians

(1) This section applies if, under a power conferred by Part IV or any other enactment or any provision of subordinate legislation, or by the trust instrument, a person other than a trustee has been –

(a) authorised to exercise functions as an agent of the trustees, or
(b) appointed to act as a nominee or custodian.

(2) The trustees may remunerate the agent, nominee or custodian out of the trust funds for services if –

(a) he is engaged on terms entitling him to be remunerated for those services, and
(b) the amount does not exceed such remuneration as is reasonable in the circumstances for the provision of those services by him to or on behalf of that trust.

(3) The trustees may reimburse the agent, nominee or custodian out of the trust funds for any expenses properly incurred by him in exercising functions as an agent, nominee or custodian.

33 Application

(1) Subject to subsection (2), sections 28, 29, 31 and 32 apply in relation to services provided to or on behalf of, or (as the case may be) expenses incurred on or after their commencement on behalf of, trusts whenever created.

(2) Nothing in section 28 or 29 is to be treated as affecting the operation of –

(a) section 15 of the Wills Act 1837, or
(b) section 34(3) of the Administration of Estates Act 1925,

in relation to any death occurring before the commencement of section 28 or (as the case may be) section 29.

PART VI

MISCELLANEOUS AND SUPPLEMENTARY

34 Power to insure

(1) For section 19 of the Trustee Act 1925 (power to insure) substitute –

'19   Power to insure

(1) A trustee may –

(a) insure any property which is subject to the trust against risks of loss or damage due to any event, and
(b) pay the premiums out of the trust funds.

(2) In the case of property held on a bare trust, the power to insure is subject to any direction given by the beneficiary or each of the beneficiaries –

(a) that any property specified in the direction is not to be insured;
(b) that any property specified in the direction is not to be insured except on such conditions as may be so specified.

(3) Property is held on a bare trust if it is held on trust for –

(a) a beneficiary who is of full age and capacity and absolutely entitled to the property subject to the trust, or
(b) beneficiaries each of whom is of full age and capacity and who (taken together) are absolutely entitled to the property subject to the trust.

(4) If a direction under subsection (2) of this section is given, the power to insure, so far as it is subject to the direction, ceases to be a delegable function for the purposes of section 11 of the Trustee act 2000 (power to employ agents).

(5) In this section "trust funds" means any income or capital funds of the trust.'

(2) In section 20(1) of the Trustee Act 1925 (application of insurance money) omit 'whether by fire or otherwise'.

(3) The amendments made by this section apply in relation to trusts whether created before or after its commencement.

35   Personal representatives

(1) Subject to the following provisions of this section, this Act applies in relation to a personal representative administering an estate according to the law as it applies to a trustee carrying out a trust for beneficiaries.

(2) For this purpose this Act is to be read with the appropriate modifications and in particular –

(a) references to the trust instrument are to be read as references to the will,
(b) references to a beneficiary or to beneficiaries, apart from the reference to a beneficiary in section 8(1)(b), are to be read as references to a person or the persons interested in the due administration of the estate, and
(c) the reference to a beneficiary in section 8(1)(b) is to be read as a reference to a person who under the will of the deceased or under the law relating to intestacy is beneficially interested in the estate.

(3) Remuneration to which a personal representative is entitled under section 28 or 29 is to be treated as an administration expense for the purposes of –

(a) section 34(3) of the Administration of Estates Act 1925 (order in which estate to be paid out), and

(b) any provision giving reasonable administration expenses priority over the preferential debts listed in Schedule 6 to the Insolvency Act 1986.

(4) Nothing in subsection (3) is to be treated as affecting the operation of the provisions mentioned in paragraphs (a) and (b) of that subsection in relation to any death occurring before the commencement of this section.

36 Pension schemes

(1) In this section 'pension scheme' means an occupational pension scheme (within the meaning of the Pension Schemes Act 1993) established under a trust and subject to the law of England and Wales.

(2) Part I does not apply in so far as it imposes a duty of care in relation to –

(a) the functions described in paragraphs 1 and 2 of Schedule 1, or

(b) the functions described in paragraph 3 of that Schedule to the extent that they relate to trustees –
  (i) authorising a person to exercise their functions with respect to investment, or
  (ii) appointing a person to act as their nominee or custodian.

(3) Nothing in Part II or III applies to the trustees of any pension scheme.

(4) Part IV applies to the trustees of a pension scheme subject to the restrictions in subsections (5) to (8).

(5) The trustees of a pension scheme may not under Part IV authorise any person to exercise any functions relating to investment as their agent.

(6) The trustees of a pension scheme may not under Part IV authorise a person who is –

(a) an employer in relation to the scheme, or

(b) connected with or an associate of such an employer,

to exercise any of their functions as their agent.

(7) For the purposes of subsection (6) –

(a) 'employer', in relation to a scheme, has the same meaning as in the Pensions Act 1995;

(b) sections 249 and 435 of the Insolvency Act 1986 apply for the purpose of determining whether a person is connected with or an associate of an employer.

(8) Sections 16 to 20 (powers to appoint nominees and custodians) do not apply to the trustees of a pension scheme.

37   Authorised unit trusts

(1)   Parts II to IV do not apply to trustees of authorised unit trusts.

(2)   'Authorised unit trust' means a unit trust scheme in the case of which an order under section 78 of the Financial Services Act 1986 is in force.

38   Common investment schemes for charities etc

Parts II to IV do not apply to –

-   (a)   trustees managing a fund under a common investment scheme made, or having effect as if made, under section 24 of the Charities Act 1993, other than such a fund the trusts of which provide that property is not to be transferred to the fund except by or on behalf of a charity the trustees of which are the trustees appointed to manage the fund, or
-   (b)   trustees managing a fund under a common deposit scheme made, or having effect as if made, under section 25 of that Act.

39   Interpretation

'asset' includes any right or interest;
'charitable trust' means a trust under which property is held for charitable purposes and 'charitable purposes' has the same meaning as in the Charities Act 1993;
'custodian trustee' has the same meaning as in the Public Trustee Act 1906;
'enactment' includes any provision of a Measure of the Church Assembly or of the General Synod of the Church of England;
'exempt charity' has the same meaning as in the Charities Act 1993;
'functions' includes powers and duties;
'legal mortgage' has the same meaning as in the Law of Property Act 1925;
'personal representative' has the same meaning as in the Trustee Act 1925;
'settled land' has the same meaning as in the Settled Land Act 1925;
'trust corporation' has the same meaning as in the Trustee Act 1925;
'trust funds' means income or capital funds of the trust.

(2)   In this Act the expressions listed below are defined or otherwise explained by the provisions indicated –

asset management functions	section 15(5)
custodian	section 17(2)
the duty of care	section 1(2)
the general power of investment	section 3(2)
lay trustee	section 28(6)
power of intervention	section 22(4)
the standard investment criteria	section 4(3)
subordinate legislation	section 6(3)
trustee acting in a professional capacity	section 28(5)
trust instrument	sections 6(2) and 35(2)(a)

40 Minor and consequential amendments etc

(1) Schedule 2 (minor and consequential amendments) shall have effect.

(2) Schedule 3 (transitional provisions and savings) shall have effect.

(3) Schedule 4 (repeals) shall have effect.

41 Power to amend other Acts

(1) A Minister of the Crown may by order make such amendments of any Act, including an Act extending to places outside England and Wales, as appear to him appropriate in consequence of or in connection with Part II or III.

(2) Before exercising the power under subsection (1) in relation to a local, personal or private Act, the Minister must consult any person who appears to him to be affected by any proposed amendment.

(3) An order under this section may –

    (a) contain such transitional provisions and savings as the Minister thinks fit;
    (b) make different provision for different purposes.

(4) The power to make an order under this section is exercisable by statutory instrument which shall be subject to annulment in pursuance of a resolution of either House of Parliament.

(5) 'Minister of the Crown' has the same meaning as in the Ministers of the Crown Act 1975.

42 Commencement and extent

(1) Section 41, this section and section 43 shall come into force on the day on which this Act is passed.

(2) The remaining provisions of this Act shall come into force on such day as the Lord Chancellor may appoint by order made by statutory instrument; and different days may be so appointed for different purposes.

(3) An order under subsection (2) may contain such transitional provisions and savings as the Lord Chancellor considers appropriate in connection with the order.

(4) Subject to section 41(1) and subsection (5), this Act extends to England and Wales only.

(5) An amendment or repeal in Part II or III of Schedule 2 or Part II of Schedule 4 has the same extent as the provision amended or repealed.

43 Short title

This Act may be cited as the Trustee Act 2000.

SCHEDULES

SCHEDULE 1

APPLICATION OF DUTY OF CARE

Investment

1. The duty of care applies to a trustee –

    (a) when exercising the general power of investment or any other power of investment, however conferred;
    (b) when carrying out a duty to which he is subject under section 4 or 5 (duties relating to the exercise of a power of investment or to the review of investments).

Acquisition of land

2. The duty of care applies to a trustee –

    (a) when exercising the power under section 8 to acquire land;
    (b) when exercising any other power to acquire land, however conferred;
    (c) when exercising any power in relation to land acquired under a power mentioned in sub-paragraph (a) or (b).

Agents, nominees and custodians

3.—(1) The duty of care applies to a trustee –

    (a) when entering into arrangements under which a person is authorised under section 11 to exercise functions as an agent;
    (b) when entering into arrangements under which a person is appointed under section 16 to act as a nominee;
    (c) when entering into arrangements under which a person is appointed under section 17 or 18 to act as a custodian;
    (d) when entering into arrangements under which, under any other power, however conferred, a person is authorised to exercise functions as an agent or is appointed to act as a nominee or custodian;
    (e) when carrying out his duties under section 22 (review of agent, nominee or custodian, etc).

(2) For the purposes of sub-paragraph (1), entering into arrangements under which a person is authorised to exercise functions or is appointed to act as a nominee or custodian includes, in particular –

    (a) selecting the person who is to act,
    (b) determining any terms on which he is to act, and
    (c) if the person is being authorised to exercise asset management functions, the preparation of a policy statement under section 15.

Compounding of liabilities

4. The duty of care applies to a trustee –

    (a) when exercising the power under section 15 of the Trustee Act 1925 to do any of the things referred to in that section;

    (b) when exercising any corresponding power, however conferred.

Insurance

5. The duty of care applies to a trustee –

    (a) when exercising the power under section 19 of the Trustee Act 1925 to insure property;

    (b) when exercising any corresponding power, however conferred.

Reversionary interests, valuations and audit

6. The duty of care applies to a trustee –

    (a) when exercising the power under section 22(1) or (3) of the Trustee Act 1925 to do any of the things referred to there;

    (b) when exercising any corresponding power, however conferred.

Exclusion of duty of care

7. The duty of care does not apply if or in so far as it appears from the trust instrument that the duty is not meant to apply.

SCHEDULE 2

MINOR AND CONSEQUENTIAL AMENDMENTS

PART I

THE TRUSTEE INVESTMENTS ACT 1961 AND THE CHARITIES ACT 1993

The Trustee Investments Act 1961 (c 62)

1.—(1) Sections 1, 2, 5, 6, 12, 13 and 15 shall cease to have effect, except in so far as they are applied by or under any other enactment.

(2) Section 3 and Schedules 2 and 3 shall cease to have effect, except in so far as they relate to a trustee having a power of investment conferred on him under an enactment –

    (a) which was passed before the passing of the 1961 Act, and

    (b) which is not amended by this Schedule.

(3) Omit –

    (a) sections 8 and 9,

(b) paragraph 1(1) of Schedule 4, and

(c) section 16(1), in so far as it relates to paragraph 1(1) of Schedule 4.

The Charities Act 1993 (c 10)

2.—(1) Omit sections 70 and 71.

(2) In section 86(2) in paragraph (a) –

(a) omit '70', and

(b) at the end insert 'or'.

(3) Omit section 86(2)(b).

PART II

OTHER PUBLIC GENERAL ACTS

The Places of Worship Sites Act 1873 (c 50)

3. In section 2 (payment of purchase money, etc) for 'shall be invested upon such securities or investments as would for the time being be authorised by statute or the Court of Chancery' substitute 'shall be invested under the general power of investment in section 3 of the Trustee Act 2000'.

The Technical and Industrial Institutions Act 1892 (c 29)

4. In section 9 (investment powers relating to proceeds of sale of land acquired under the Act) for subsection (5) substitute –

'(5) Money arising by sale may, until reinvested in the purchase of land, be invested –

(a) in the names of the governing body, in any investments in which trustees may invest under the general power of investment in section 3 of the Trustee Act 2000 (as restricted by sections 4 and 5 of that Act), or

(b) under the general power of investment in section 3 of that Act, by trustees for the governing body or by a person authorised by the trustees under that Act to invest as an agent of the trustees.

(6) Any profits from investments under subsection (5) shall be invested in the same way and added to capital until the capital is reinvested in the purchase of land.'

The Duchy of Cornwall Management Act 1893 (c 20)

5. The 1893 Act is hereby repealed.

The Duchy of Lancaster Act 1920 (c 51)

6. In section 1 (extension of powers of investment of funds of Duchy of Lancaster) for 'in any of the investments specified in paragraph (a) of section one of the

Trustees Act 1893 and any enactment amending or extending that paragraph' substitute 'under the general power of investment in section 3 of the Trustee Act 2000 (as restricted by sections 4 and 5 of that Act)'.

The Settled Land Act 1925 (c 18)

7. In section 21 (absolute owners subject to certain interests to have the powers of tenant for life), in subsection (1)(d) for 'income thereof' substitute 'resultant profits'.

8. In section 39 (regulations respecting sales), in subsection (2), in the proviso, for the words from 'accumulate' to the end of the subsection substitute 'accumulate the profits from the capital money by investing them and any resulting profits under the general power of investment in section 3 of the Trustee Act 2000 and shall add the accumulations to capital.'

9. In section 73 (modes of investment or application), in subsection (1) for paragraph (i) substitute –

'(i)   In investment in securities either under the general power of investment in section 3 of the Trustee Act 2000 or under a power to invest conferred on the trustees of the settlement by the settlement;'.

10.—(1) In section 75 (regulations respecting investment, devolution, and income of securities etc), for subsection (2) substitute –

'(2) Subject to Part IV of the Trustee Act 2000, to section 75A of this Act and to the following provisions of this section –

(a) the investment or other application by the trustees shall be made according to the discretion of the trustees, but subject to any consent required or direction given by the settlement with respect to the investment or other application by the trustees of trust money of the settlement, and

(b) any investment shall be in the names or under the control of the trustees.'

(2) For subsection (4) of that section substitute –

'(4) The trustees, in exercising their power to invest or apply capital money, shall –

(a) so far as practicable, consult the tenant for life; and

(b) so far as consistent with the general interest of the settlement, give effect to his wishes.

(4A) Any investment or other application of capital money under the direction of the court shall not during the subsistence of the beneficial interest of the tenant for life be altered without his consent.

(4B) The trustees may not under section 11 of the Trustee Act 2000 authorise a person to exercise their functions with respect to the investment or application of capital money on terms that prevent them from complying with subsection (4) of this section.

(4C) A person who is authorised under section 11 of the Trustee Act 2000 to exercise any of their functions with respect to the investment or application of capital money is not subject to subsection (4) of this section.'

(3) Nothing in this paragraph affects the operation of section 75 in relation to directions of the tenant for life given, but not acted upon by the trustees, before the commencement of this paragraph.

11. After section 75 insert –

'75A   Power to accept charge as security for part payment for land sold

(1) Where –

  (a) land subject to the settlement is sold by the tenant for life or statutory owner, for an estate in fee simple or a term having at least five hundred years to run, and
  (b) the proceeds of sale are liable to be invested.

the tenant for life or statutory owner may, with the consent of the trustees of the settlement, contract that the payment of any part, not exceeding two-thirds, of the purchase money shall be secured by a charge by way of legal mortgage of the land sold, with or without the security of any other property.

(2) If any buildings are comprised in the property secured by the charge, the charge must contain a covenant by the mortgagor to keep them insured for their full value against loss or damage due to any event.

(3) A person exercising the power under subsection (1) of this section, or giving consent for the purposes of that subsection –

  (a) is not required to comply with section 5 of the Trustee Act 2000 before giving his consent, and
  (b) is not liable for any loss incurred merely because the security is insufficient at the date of the charge.

(4) The power under subsection (1) of this section is exercisable subject to the consent of any person whose consent to a change of investment is required by the instrument, if any, creating the trust.

(5) Where the sale referred to in subsection (1) of this section is made under the order of the court, the power under that subsection applies only if and as far as the court may by order direct.'

12. Omit section 96 (protection of each trustee individually).

13. In section 98 (protection of trustees in particular cases), omit subsections (1) and (2).

14. Omit section 100 (trustees' reimbursements).

15. In section 102 (management of land during minority or pending contingency), in subsection (2) for paragraph (e) substitute –

'(e) to insure against risks of loss or damage due to any event under section 19 of the Trustee Act 1925;'.

16.—(1) In section 104 (powers of tenant for life not assignable etc) –

(a) in subsection (3)(b) omit 'authorised by statute for the investment of trust money', and

(b) in subsection (4)(b) for the words from 'no investment' to 'trust money;' substitute 'the consent of the assignee shall be required to an investment of capital money for the time being affected by the assignment in investments other than securities, and to any application of such capital money;'.

(2) Sub-paragraph (1) applies to the determination on or after the commencement of that sub-paragraph of whether an assignee's consent is required to the investment or application of capital money.

17. In section 107 (tenant for life deemed to be in the position and to have the duties and liabilities of a trustee, etc) after subsection (1) insert –

'(1A) The following provisions apply to the tenant for life as they apply to the trustees of the settlement –

(a) sections 11, 13 to 15 and 21 to 23 of the Trustee Act 2000 (power to employ agents subject to certain restrictions),

(b) section 32 of that Act (remuneration and expenses of agents etc),

(c) section 19 of the Trustee Act 1925 (power to insure), and

(d) in so far as they relate to the provisions mentioned in paragraphs (a) and (c), Part I of, and Schedule 1 to, the Trustee Act 2000 (the duty of care).'

The Trustee Act 1925 (c 19)

18. Omit Part I (investments).

19. In section 14 (power of trustees to give receipts) in subsection (1) after 'securities,' insert 'investments'.

20. In section 15 (power to compound liabilities), for 'in good faith' substitute 'if he has or they have discharged the duty of care set out in section 1(1) of the Trustee Act 2000'.

21. Omit section 21 (deposit of documents for safe custody).

22. In section 22 (reversionary interests, valuations, and audit) –

(a) in subsection (1), for 'in good faith' substitute 'if they have discharged the duty of care set out in section (1) of the Trustee Act 2000', and

(b) in subsection (3), omit 'in good faith' and at the end insert 'if the trustees have discharged the duty of care set out in section 1(1) of the Trustee Act 2000'.

23. Omit section 23 (power to employ agents).

24. Omit section 30 (implied indemnity of trustees).

25. In section 31(2) (power to invest income during minority) for 'in the way of compound interest by investing the same and the resulting income thereof' substitute 'by investing it, and any profits from so investing it'.

The Land Registration Act 1925 (c 21)

26. In section 94(1) (registered land subject to a trust to be registered in the names of the trustees), at the end insert 'or in the name of a nominee appointed under section 16 of the Trustee Act 2000'.

The Administration of Estates Act 1925 (c 23)

27. In section 33, in subsection (3) (investment during minority of beneficiary or the subsistence of a life interest) for the words from 'in any investments for the time being authorised by statute' to the end of the subsection substitute 'under the Trustee Act 2000.'

28. In section 39 (powers of management) after subsection (1) insert –

'(1A) Subsection (1) of this section is without prejudice to the powers conferred on personal representatives by the Trustee Act 2000.'

The Universities and College Estates Act 1925 (c 24)

29. In section 26 (modes of application of capital money) in subsection (1) for paragraph (i) substitute –

'(i)   In investments in which trustees may invest under the general power of investment in section 3 of the Trustee Act 2000 (as restricted by sections 4 and 5 of that Act);'.

The Regimental Charitable Funds Act 1935 (c 11)

30. In section 2(1) (application of funds held on account of regimental charitable funds) –

(a)   in paragraph (a) for 'in some manner' to 'trusts' substitute 'under the general power of investment in section 3 of the Trustee Act 2000';
(b)   in paragraph (b) after 'the income' insert 'or the other profits'.

The Agricultural Marketing Act 1958 (c 47)

31.—(1) In section 16 (investment of surplus funds of boards) for paragraph (a) substitute –

'(a)   the moneys of the board not for the time being required by them for the purposes of their functions are not, except with the approval of the Minister, invested otherwise than in investments in which trustees may invest under the general power of investment in section 3 of the Trustee Act 2000 (as restricted by sections 4 and 5 of that Act); and'.

(2) Any scheme made under the 1958 Act and in effect before the day on which sub-paragraph (1) comes into force shall be treated, in relation to the making of investments on and after that day, as including provision permitting investment by the board in accordance with section 16(a) of the 1958 Act as amended by sub-paragraph (1).

The Horticulture Act 1960 (c 22)

32. In section 13 (miscellaneous financial powers of organisations promoting home-grown produce) for subsection (3) substitute –

'(3) A relevant organisation may invest any of its surplus money which is not for the time being required for any other purpose in any investments in which trustees may invest under the general power of investment in section 3 of the Trustee Act 2000 (as restricted by sections 4 and 5 of that Act)'.

The House of Commons Members' Fund Act 1962 (c 53)

33.—(1) In section 1 (powers of investment of trustees of House of Commons Members' Fund) –

(a) in subsection (2) omit 'Subject to the following provisions of this section';
(b) omit subsections (3) to (5).

(2) In section 2 (interpretation etc) omit subsection (1).

The Betting, Gaming and Lotteries Act 1963 (c 2)

34. In section 25(1) (general powers and duties of the Horserace Betting Levy Board) for paragraph (e) substitute –

'(e) to make such other investments as –
    (i) they judge desirable for the proper conduct of their affairs, and
    (ii) a trustee would be able to make under the general power of investment in section 3 of the Trustee Act 2000 (as restricted by sections 4 and 5 of that Act);'.

The Cereals Marketing Act 1965 (c 14)

35.—(1) In section 18, in subsection (2) (Home-Grown Cereals Authority's power to invest reserve funds) for 'in accordance with the next following subsection' substitute 'in any investments in which trustees may invest under the general power of investment in section 3 of the Trustee Act 2000 (as restricted by sections 4 and 5 of that Act).'

(2) Omit section 18(3).

The Agriculture Act 1967 (c 22)

36.—(1) In section 18, in subsection (2) (Meat and Livestock Commission's power to invest reserve fund) for 'in accordance with the next following subsection' substitute 'in any investments in which trustees may invest under the general power of investment in section 3 of the Trustee Act 2000 (as restricted by sections 4 and 5 of that Act).'

(2) Omit section 18(3).

The Solicitors Act 1974 (c 47)

37. In Schedule 2, for paragraph 3 (power of Law Society to invest) substitute –

'3. The Society may invest any money which forms part of the fund in any investments in which trustees may invest under the general power of investment in section 3 of the Trustee Act 2000 (as restricted by sections 4 and 5 of that Act).'

The Policyholders Protection Act 1975 (c 75)

38. In Schedule 1, in paragraph 7, for sub-paragraph (1) (power of Policyholders Protection Board to invest) substitute –

'(1) The Board may invest funds held by them which appear to them to be surplus to their requirements for the time being –

    (a) in any investments in which trustees may invest under the general power of investment in section 3 of the Trustee act 2000 (as restricted by sections 4 and 5 of that Act); or

    (b) in any investment approved for the purpose by the Treasury.'

The National Heritage Act 1980 (c 17)

39. In section 6 for subsection (3) (powers of investment of Trustees of National Heritage Memorial Fund) substitute –

'(3) The Trustees may invest any sums to which subsection (2) does not apply in any investments in which trustees may invest under the general power of investment in section 3 of the Trustee Act 2000 (as restricted by sections 4 and 5 of that Act).'

The Licensing (Alcohol Education and Research) Act 1981 (c 28)

40. In section 7 (powers of investment of Alcohol Education and Research Council) for subsection (5) substitute –

'(5) Any sums in the Fund which are not immediately required for any other purpose may be invested by the Council in any investments in which trustees may invest under the general power of investment in section 3 of the Trustee Act 2000 (as restricted by sections 4 and 5 of that Act).'

The Fisheries Act 1981 (c 29)

41. For section 10 (powers of investment of Sea Fish Industry Authority) substitute –

'Investment of reserve funds

10. Any money of the Authority which is not immediately required for any other purpose may be invested by the Authority in any investments in which trustees may invest under the general power of investment in section 3 of the Trustee Act 2000 (as restricted by sections 4 and 5 of that Act)'.

The Duchy of Cornwall Management Act 1982 (c 47)

42. For section 1 (powers of investment of Duchy property) substitute –

'Powers of investment of Duchy property

1. The power of investment conferred by the Duchy of Cornwall Management Act 1863 includes power to invest in any investments in which trustees may invest under the general power of investment in section 3 of the Trustee Act 2000 (as restricted by sections 4 and 5 of that Act).'

43. In –

   (a) section 6(3) (Duchy of Cornwall Management Acts extended in relation to banking), and
   (b) section 11(2) (collective citation of Duchy of Cornwall Management Acts),

for 'Duchy of Cornwall Management Acts 1868 to 1893' substitute 'Duchy of Cornwall Management Acts 1863 to 1868'.

The Administration of Justice Act 1982 (c 53)

44. In section 42 (common investment schemes) in subsection (6) for paragraph (a) substitute –

   '(a) he may invest trust money in shares in the fund without obtaining and considering advice on whether to make such an investment; and'.

The Trusts of Land and Appointment of Trustees Act 1996 (c 47)

45.—(1) In section 6 (general powers of trustees), in subsection (3) for 'purchase a legal estate in any land in England and Wales' substitute 'acquire land under the power conferred by section 8 of the Trustee Act 2000.'

(2) Omit subsection (4) of that section.

(3) After subsection (8) of that section insert –

   '(9) The duty of care under section 1 of the Trustee Act 2000 applies to trustees of land when exercising the powers conferred by this section.'

46. In section 9 (delegation by trustees) omit subsection (8).

47. After section 9 insert –

'9A Duties of trustees in connection with delegation etc

(1) The duty of care under section 1 of the Trustee Act 200 applies to trustees of land in deciding whether to delegate any of their functions under section 9.

(2) Subsection (3) applies if the trustees of land –

   (a) delegate any of their functions under section 9, and

(b) the delegation is not irrevocable.

(3) While the delegation continues, the trustees –

    (a) must keep the delegation under review,

    (b) if circumstances make it appropriate to do so, must consider whether there is a need to exercise any power of intervention that they have, and

    (c) if they consider that there is a need to exercise such a power, must do so.

(4) "Power of intervention" includes –

    (a) a power to give directions to the beneficiary;

    (b) a power to revoke the delegation.

(5) The duty of care under section 1 of the 2000 Act applies to trustees in carrying out any duty under subsection (3).

(6) A trustee of land is not liable for any act or default of the beneficiary, or beneficiaries, unless the trustee fails to comply with the duty of care in deciding to delegate any of the trustees' functions under section 9 or in carrying out any duty under subsection (3).

(7) Neither this section nor the repeal of section 9(8) by the Trustee Act 2000 affects the operation after the commencement of this section of any delegation effected before that commencement.'

48. Omit section 17(1) (application of section 6(3) in relation to trustees of proceeds of sale of land).

49. In Schedule 3 (consequential amendments) omit paragraph 3(4) (amendment of section 19(1) and (2) of Trustee Act 1925).

PART III

MEASURES

The Ecclesiastical Dilapidations Measure 1923 (No 3)

50. In section 52, in subsection (5) (investment of sums held in relation to repair of chancels) –

    (a) for 'in any investment permitted by law for the investment of trust funds, and the yearly income resulting therefrom shall be applied,' substitute 'in any investments in which trustees may invest under the general power of investment in section 3 of the Trustee Act 2000, and the annual profits from the investments shall be applied'; and

    (b) in paragraph (iii) for 'any residue of the said income not applied as aforesaid in any year' substitute 'any residue of the profits from the investments not applied in any year.'

The Diocesan Stipends Funds Measure 1953 (No 2)

51. In section 4 (application of moneys credited to capital accounts) in subsection (1) for paragraph (bc) substitute –

'(bc) investment in any investments in which trustees may invest under the general power of investment in section 3 of the Trustee Act 2000 (as restricted by sections 4 and 5 of that Act);'.

The Church Funds Investment Measure 1958 (No 1)

52. In the Schedule, in paragraph 21 (range of investments of deposit fund) for paragraphs (a) to (d) of sub-paragraph (1) substitute –

'(aa)   In any investments in which trustees may invest under the general power of investment in section 3 of the Trustee Act 2000 (as restricted by sections 4 and 5 of that Act);'.

The Clergy Pensions Measure 1961 (No 3)

53.—(1) In section 32 (investment powers of Board), in subsection (1), for paragraph (a) substitute –

'(a)   in any investments in which trustees may invest under the general power of investment in section 3 of the Trustee Act 2000 (as restricted by sections 4 and 5 of that Act);'.

(2) Omit subsection (3) of that section.

The Repair of Benefice Buildings Measure 1972 (No 2)

54. In section 17, in subsection (2) (diocesan parsonages fund's power of investment), for 'who shall have the same powers of investment as trustees of trust funds:' substitute 'who shall have the same power as trustees to invest in any investments in which trustees may invest under the general power of investment in section 3 of the Trustee Act 2000 (as restricted by sections 4 and 5 of that Act).'

The Pastoral Measure 1983 (No 1)

55. In section 44, for subsection (6) (Redundant Churches Fund's power of investment) substitute –

'(6) The powers to invest any such sums are –

(a)   power to invest in investments in which trustees may invest under the general power of investment in section 3 of the Trustee Act 2000 (as restricted by sections 4 and 5 of that Act); and

(b)   power to invest in the investments referred to in paragraph 21(1)(e) and (f) of the Schedule to the Church Funds Investment Measure 1958.'

The Church of England (Pensions) Measure 1988 (No 4)

56. Omit section 14(b) (amendment of section 32(3) of the Clergy Pensions Measure 1961).

The Cathedrals Measure 1999 (No 1)

57. In section 16 (cathedral moneys: investment powers, etc), in subsection (1) –

(a) for paragraph (c) substitute –

'(c) power to invest in any investments in which trustees may invest under the general power of investment in section 3 of the Trustee Act 2000 (as restricted by sections 4 and 5 of that Act),', and

(b) omit the words from 'and the powers' to the end of the subsection.

SCHEDULE 3

TRANSITIONAL PROVISIONS AND SAVINGS

The Trustee Act 1925 (c 19)

1.—(1) Sub-paragraph (2) applies if, immediately before the day on which Part IV of this Act comes into force, a banker or banking company holds any bearer securities deposited with him under section 7(1) of the 1925 Act (investment in bearer securities).

(2) On and after the day on which Part IV comes into force, the banker or banking company shall be treated as if he had been appointed as custodian of the securities under section 18.

2. The repeal of section 8 of the 1925 Act (loans and investments by trustees not chargeable as breaches of trust) does not affect the operation of that section in relation to loans or investments made before the coming into force of that repeal.

3. The repeal of section 9 of the 1925 Act (liability for loss by reason of improper investment) does not affect the operation of that section in relation to any advance of trust money made before the coming into force of that repeal.

4.—(1) Sub-paragraph (2) applies if, immediately before the day on which Part IV of this Act comes into force, a banker or banking company holds any documents deposited with him under section 21 of the 1925 Act (deposit of documents for safe custody).

(2) On and after the day on which Part IV comes into force, the banker or banking company shall be treated as if he had been appointed as custodian of the documents under section 17.

5.—(1) Sub-paragraph (2) applies if, immediately before the day on which Part IV of this Act comes into force, a person has been appointed to act as or be an agent or attorney under section 23(1) or (3) of the 1925 Act (general power to employ agents etc).

(2) On and after the day on which Part IV comes into force, the agent shall be treated as if he had been authorised to exercise functions as an agent under section 11 (and, if appropriate, as if he had also been appointed under that Part to act as a custodian or nominee).

6. The repeal of section 23(2) of the 1925 Act (power to employ agents in respect of property outside the United Kingdom) does not affect the operation after the commencement of the repeal of an appointment made before that commencement.

The Trustee Investments Act 1961 (c 62)

7.—(1) A trustee shall not be liable for breach of trust merely because he continues to hold an investment acquired by virtue of paragraph 14 of Part II of Schedule 1 to the 1961 Act (perpetual rent-charges etc).

(2) A person who –

(a) is not a trustee,
(b) before the commencement of Part II of this Act had powers to invest in the investments described in paragraph 14 of Part II of Schedule 1 to the 1961 Act, and
(c) on that commencement acquired the general power of investment,

shall not be treated as exceeding his powers of investment merely because he continues to hold an investment acquired by virtue of that paragraph.

The Cathedrals Measure 1963 (No 2)

8. While section 21 of the Cathedrals Measure 1963 (investment powers, etc of capitular bodies) continues to apply in relation to any cathedral, that section shall have effect as if –

(a) in subsection (1), for paragraph (c) and the words from 'and the powers' to the end of the subsection there were substituted –

'(c) power to invest in any investments in which trustees may invest under the general power of investment in section 3 of the Trustee Act 2000 (as restricted by sections 4 and 5 of that Act).', and

(b) in subsection (5), for 'subsections (2) and (3) of section six of the Trustee Investments Act 1961' there were substituted 'section 5 of the Trustee Act 2000'.

SCHEDULE 4

REPEALS

PART I

THE TRUSTEE INVESTMENTS ACT 1961 AND THE CHARITIES ACT 1993

Chapter	Short title	Extent of repeal
1961 c 62	The Trustee Investments Act 1961	Sections 1 to 3, 5, 6, 8, 9, 12, 13, 15 and 16(1) Schedules 2 and 3 In Schedule 4, paragraph 1(1)
1993 c 10	The Charities Act 1993	Sections 70 and 71 In section 86(2) in paragraph (a), '70' and paragraph (b)

Note: the repeals in this Part of this Schedule have effect in accordance with Part I of Schedule 2.

PART II

OTHER APPEALS

Chapter	Short title	Extent of repeal
1893 c 20	The Duchy of Cornwall Management Act 1893	The whole Act
1925 c 18	The Settled Land Act 1925	Section 96 Section 98(1) and (2) Section 100 In section 104(3)(b) the words 'authorised by statute for the investment of trust money'
1925 c 19	The Trustee Act 1925	Part I In section 20(1) the words 'whether by fire or otherwise' Sections 21, 23 and 30
1961 No 3	The Clergy Pensions Measure 1961	Section 32(3)

Chapter	Short title	Extent of repeal
1962 c 53	The House of Commons Members' Fund Act 1962	In section 1, in subsection (2) the words 'Subject to the following provisions of this section' and subsections (3) to (5) Section 2(1)
1965 c 14	The Cereals Marketing Act 1965	Section 18(3)
1967 c 22	The Agriculture Act 1967	Section 18(3)
1988 No 4	The Church of England (Pensions) Measure 1988	Section 14(b)
1996 c 47	The Trusts of Land and Appointment of Trustees Act 1996	Section 6(4) Section 9(8) Section 17(1) In Schedule 3, paragraph 3(4)
1999 No 1	The Cathedrals Measure 1999	In section 16(1), the words from 'and the powers' to the end of the subsection

Appendix II

PARLIAMENTARY STAGES OF THE TRUSTEE ACT

HOUSE OF LORDS

1st Reading: HL Deb, vol 608, 20 January 2000, col 1245.
2nd Reading: HL Deb, vol 612, 14 April 2000, cols 373–397.
Committee: HL Deb, vol 613, 7 June 2000, cols CWH 1–CWH 16.
Report: HL Deb, vol 614, 23 June 2000, cols 561–564.
3rd Reading: HL Deb, vol 614, 29 June 2000, cols 1070–1072.

HOUSE OF COMMONS

1st Reading: 29 June 2000.
2nd Reading: HC Deb, vol 354, 26 July 2000, col 1132.
Committee: Standing Committee A, 26 and 30 October 2000.
Report: HC Deb, vol 356, 8 November 2000, col 350.
3rd Reading: HC Deb, vol 356, 8 November 2000, cols 350–357.

ROYAL ASSENT

23 November 2000.

COMMENCEMENT

1 February 2001 (anticipated).

Appendix III

PRECEDENTS

FORM A: INCLUSION OF STATUTORY POWER IN INVESTMENT

The Trustees shall invest the Trust Fund[1] in accordance with the powers conferred on them by the Trustee Act 2000 or any statutory modification of it for the time being in force [and for the avoidance of doubt the Trustees shall be entitled to invest in assets whether income producing or not][2] [PROVIDED THAT the Trustees shall not invest in any investments set out in the Schedule hereto][3].

FORM B: INVESTMENT ON ETHICAL GROUNDS

The Trustees shall only invest the Trust Fund in investments [which they in their absolute discretion consider to be acceptable on ethical grounds][4] or [which do not directly or indirectly involve investment in, eg the Tobacco industry/petrol companies][5] without being liable for any loss which might thereby occur to the Trust Fund.

FORM C: CLAUSE EXCLUDING STATUTORY POWER OF INVESTMENT

The powers of investment conferred on trustees by the Trustee Act 2000 shall not apply to this [Settlement] [Will][6].

---

1   It is assumed in this and the following precedents that this will be defined elsewhere in the settlement or will.
2   For inclusion if it is to be made clear that not only income-producing assets are to be regarded as investments.
3   For inclusion if the settlor or testator wishes to restrict the powers in some way.
4   It would be appropriate to include with a settlement or will containing such a clause a letter of wishes on the part of the settlor or testator indicating the ethical considerations to be taken into account.
5   Although the draftsman may think that this alternative is more precise, it can be difficult to draft in sufficiently clear terms to ensure that the trustees are sure what they must avoid by way of investment. The first alternative and a letter of wishes is probably to be preferred.
6   The inclusion in the settlement or will of an express power of investment is enough to exclude the statutory power, but the draftsman may wish to avoid any doubt by the inclusion of this clause.

FORM D: CLAUSE EXCLUDING POWER TO ACQUIRE LAND

The powers conferred on Trustees to acquire land by section 8 of the Trustee Act 2000 shall not apply to this [Settlement] [Will].

FORM E: STANDARD PROFESSIONAL CHARGING CLAUSE

Any Trustee (other than the Settlor and any spouse of the Settlor) being a solicitor or other person engaged in any profession or business shall be entitled to charge and be paid all usual professional or other charges for business done by him or his firm or company in relation to the [trusts of this Settlement] [administration of my estate or the provisions of this Will or any codicil to it] including work outside the ordinary course of his profession or business and work which he could or should have done personally had he not been so engaged.

FORM F: AGREEMENT OF TRUSTEES IN WRITING THAT PROFESSIONAL TRUSTEE SHOULD RECEIVE REMUNERATION

THIS AGREEMENT is made on the ... day of ... between AB(1) CD(2) and EF(3)

Recitals

Whereas:

(1) AB, CD and EF are the present trustees of a settlement ('the Settlement') particulars of which are set out in the Schedule hereto.
(2) AB is a solicitor and CD and EF have agreed that he should be remunerated out of the Trust Fund (as defined in the Settlement) for any services he provides to and on behalf of the trust in the manner hereinafter appearing.

Operative Parts

CD and EF hereby agree in accordance with section 29 of the Trustee Act 2000 that AB should receive reasonable remuneration[7] out of the Trust Fund for services he provides to and on behalf of the trust.

Signed etc.

---

7   Or remuneration could be specified.

FORM G: PARTICULARS OF CLAIM (HIGH COURT) ALLEGING BREACH OF THE STATUTORY DUTY OF CARE IN RESPECT OF INVESTMENT

IN THE HIGH COURT OF JUSTICE   200 [   ]CH [*number*]

CHANCERY DIVISION

In the Matter of the Trustee Act 2000

BETWEEN:

(1) A.B.
(2) C.D.

Claimants

– and –

(1) E.F.
(2) G.H.

Defendants

PARTICULARS OF CLAIM

1.   The Defendants are the trustees of a settlement (hereinafter referred to as 'the Settlement') dated [*date*] made between (1) I.J. ('the Settlor') and (2) the Defendants.

2.   The Claimants are the beneficiaries under the Settlement[8].

3.   On [*date*] the Defendants purchased 1000 ordinary shares in XYZ.com Ltd at a total cost of £90,000. The said sum represented 90% of the money subject to the trusts of the Settlement at the date of purchase. In purchasing the said shares the Defendants have acted in breach of the duty of care owed by them to the Claimants pursuant to section 1 of the Trustee Act 2000.

PARTICULARS

(i)   The Defendants failed to take or consider any or any proper advice as to the exercise of their powers of investment in accordance with the standard investment criteria.

(ii)   The Defendants failed to consider the suitability of the purchase of the said shares in XYZ.com Ltd.

(iii)   The Defendants failed consider the need to diversify the investments of the Settlement and failed to so diversify.

4.   Further and in the alternative by reason of the matters aforesaid the purchase of the said shares was in breach of trust[9].

5.   The said shares are valued at £100 at the date hereof. In the premises the Settlement has suffered a loss in the sum £89,900.

---

8   It is not necessary for all of the beneficiaries to be a party to the action. If necessary, a representation could be sought.

9   See paras **3.44** *et seq.*

AND the Claimants claim:

(i)   restoration to the funds of the Settlement of the sum of £89,900;

(ii) alternatively damages[10];

(iii) an account of what is due to the estate the subject of the Settlement for interest on the said sum of £89,900;

(iv) payment of the amount found due on taking the account referred to at (ii);

(v)   such other accounts and inquiries or further or other relief as the court shall think just.

Dated etc.

[STATEMENT OF TRUTH]

---

10   Until resolution, the question of whether a breach of the statutory duty of care gives rise to a claim for breach of statutory duty of care, it is best to seek common law damages as an alternative remedy.

FORM H: PARTICULARS OF CLAIM (COUNTY COURT) ALLEGING BREACH OF THE STATUTORY DUTY OF CARE IN RESPECT OF DELEGATION

IN THE [*Name*] COUNTY COURT Case Number:

CHANCERY BUSINESS

In the Matter of the Trustee Act 2000

BETWEEN:

(1) A.B.
(2) C.D.

Claimants

– and –

(1) E.F.
(2) G.H.

Defendants

PARTICULARS OF CLAIM

1. The Defendants are the trustees of a settlement (hereinafter referred to as 'the Settlement') dated [*date*] made between (1) I.J. ('the Settlor') and (2) the Defendants.

2. The Claimants are the beneficiaries under the Settlement[11].

3. On [*date*] the Defendants appointed a Mr X to act as their agent in respect of the investment of the monies subject to the trusts of the Settlement. Such appointment constituted a delegation of asset management functions as defined by section 15 of the Trustee Act 2000. Such delegation was in breach of the duty of care owed by the Defendants to the Claimants pursuant to section 1 of the Trustee Act 2000.

PARTICULARS

(i)   no agreement was made or evidenced in writing;
(ii) no policy statement was prepared.

4. Further the Defendants failed to review the activities of Mr X sufficiently or at all.

5. On or about [*date*] Mr X invested £10,000 being the entirety of the monies subject to the trusts of the Settlement in 1000 ordinary shares in Dodgy Limited, a company who at the time of the investment was subject to an investigation by the Department of Trade and Industry. The said shares are now worthless. In the premises the trust has suffered a loss of £10,000.

---

11   It is not necessary for all of the beneficiaries to be a party to the action. If necessary, a representation order could be sought.

AND the Claimants claim:

(i)   restoration to the funds of the Settlement of the sum of £10,000;
(ii)   alternatively damages;
(iii) an account of what is due to the estate the subject of the Settlement for interest on the said sum of £10,000;
(iv)   payment of the amount found due on taking the account referred to at (ii);
(v)   such other accounts and inquiries or further or other relief as the court shall think just.

Dated etc.

[STATEMENT OF TRUTH]

FORM I: DEFENCE TO FORM H (HIGH COURT) RELYING UPON EXEMPTION CLAUSE

IN THE HIGH COURT OF JUSTICE   200[   ]CH [*number*]

CHANCERY DIVISION

In the Matter of the Trustee Act 2000

BETWEEN:

(1) A.B.

(2) C.D.

Claimants

– and –

(1) E.F.

(2) G.H.

Defendants

DEFENCE

1. Paragraphs 1 and 2 of the Particulars of Claim are admitted.

2. The Defendants further admit the purchase of shares alleged at paragraph 3 of the Particulars of Claim but deny that they were subject to any duty of care as alleged therein.

3. Clause [*number*] of the Settlement provides as follows:

    'The duty of care pursuant to section 1 of the Trustee Act 2000 shall not apply to the trusts of this settlement.'

4. Accordingly it is denied that the Claimants are entitled to the relief claimed or any relief.

[STATEMENT OF TRUTH]

FORM J: CLAUSE EXCLUDING THE STATUTORY DUTY OF CARE

The statutory duty of care under section 1 of the Trustee Act 2000 shall not apply to this trust.

FORM K: CLAUSE LIMITING THE STANDARD OF CARE

The statutory duty of care under section 1 of the Trustee Act 2000 shall apply to this trust but my trustees (both lay and professional) shall be required to exercise such care and skill as is reasonable in the circumstances to expect from a lay trustee, and no account shall be taken of the factors contained in section 1(1)(a) or (b) of the Trustee Act 2000.

FORM L: INVESTMENT POLICY CHECKLIST

1. What restrictions should apply to the investment in terms of:
   1.1 the type of investment (eg are certain types of investment prohibited by the terms of the trust? Is it a charitable trust where investment in certain assets would be contrary to the objects of the charity? Is investment to be on a particular ethical or moral basis either authorised by the trust, or on the basis that there is no financial disadvantage to the trustee investing in such a way?)
   1.2 area of the market (similar considerations may apply as above and the trustees may wish to restrict investment in hazardous securities such as dot.com companies);
   1.3 spread of investments; the trustees' policy on diversification should be set out here.

2. Should the investment manager:
   2.1 be permitted to deal in Options, Futures and Contracts for Differences and if so for what purpose?;
   2.2 procure the exercise of voting rights on a particular basis or only with the specific instructions of the trustees;
   2.3 invest in land? If so, what sort of land? What steps does the investment manager have to take before investing in land (eg valuations, surveys).

3. In the case of a trust with a life tenant and remainderman, the policy statement should set out the need to invest in such a way that the trustees' duty to act fairly as between the life tenant and the remainderman is maintained. So for example the fund cannot be invested in such a way that the income payable to the life tenant is affected; or for example holding the balance may involve the growth of capital at the expense of income if the life tenant is well off, or alternatively the reverse if the life tenant is in need but the remainderman is relatively wealthy.

4. The policy statement should also deal with the question of tax. Factors to be dealt with include the impact of income tax, IHT and CGT on sales and purchases of investments and the effect of taxation on the way in which the appropriate balance of capital and income is achieved.

5. How often should the investment manager review the investments of the fund, and how frequently should he meet with and discuss the investments with the trustees?

6. How important is liquidity? How much of the fund should, at any one time, remain uninvested?

INDEX

References are to paragraph numbers.

Acquisition of land
  absolute owner, as   4.16, 4.20–
    4.21
  'acquire', definition of   4.11
  application of new powers   1.17–
    1.18, 4.3, 4.25–4.28
    precedent for exclusion of
      App III (Form D)
  'beneficiary', definition of   4.13–
    4.14
  duty of care   2.15–2.18, 4.22–4.24
  'freehold or leasehold land',
    definition of   4.15
  investment, as form of   4.1–4.2
  jurisdiction   4.17–4.19
  'land', definition of   1.34
  statutory duty of care   2.15–2.18,
    4.22–4.24
  strict settlements, under   4.6–4.9,
    4.29–4.36
  trusts of land, under   4.6–4.9
  trusts of personalty, under
    4.4–4.5
  UK, confinement of power to,
    4.17–4.19
Agents
  appointment   1.19–1.20, 5.9–5.15
    statutory duty of care   2.19–
      2.23, 2.55–2.59
  duties   5.26–5.34
  eligibility   5.16
  remuneration   5.20–5.24, 6.38–
    6.42
  terms of agency   5.17–5.19
Amendments and repeals   1.28–
  1.31
  application of the Act   1.10–1.13
Audit
  statutory duty of care   2.28–2.29

Bare trustees
  general power of investment,
    application of, to   3.64

insure, power to   7.7
statutory duty of care, application of,
  to   2.35

Charging clauses *see* Remuneration
Commencement of Act   1.26–1.27
Compounding of liabilities
  statutory duty of care   2.24–2.26
Constructive trustees
  general power of investment,
    application of, to   3.65
  statutory duty of care, application of,
    to   2.36
Custodians
  appointment   1.19–1.20, 5.36–
    5.39
    statutory duty of care   2.19–
      2.23, 2.55–2.59
  remuneration   5.20–5.24, 5.39,
    6.38–6.42

Definitions
  'investment'   1.34, 3.15–3.18
  'land'   1.34
  'trustee'   1.34, 2.34
Delegation *see also* Agents; Custodians;
  Nominees
  application of new powers   5.2,
    5.7–5.8
    sole trustees, to   5.47
  'asset management functions', of
    5.25
  checklist   5.49
  'delegable functions'   5.9–5.15
  duty of care   2.19–2.23, 2.55–2.59
    breach of duty, effect of   5.46
    precedent for claim alleging
      breach: App III (Form I)
  liability of trustee   5.44–5.45
  Public Trustee Act 1906, under
    the   5.5

Delegation – *cont*
    reform, need for   5.1, 5.6
    review, duty to   5.22, 5.40–5.43
    statutory duty of care   2.19–2.23,
        2.55–2.59
        breach of duty, effect of   5.46
        precedent for claim alleging
            breach: App III (Form I)
    strict settlements, under   5.8
    Trustee Act 1925, under the
        5.3–5.6
Duty of care
    common law duty   2.48–2.54
    statutory duty *see* Statutory duty of
        care

General power of investment   1.14–
    1.16, 3.11–3.14, 3.56–3.65

Implied trustees *see* Constructive
    trustees; Resulting trustees
Insurance
    application of new powers   1.22,
        7.6–7.9
    duty of care   2.27, 7.8–7.9
    duty to insure   7.10–7.14
    reform, need for   7.2
    statutory duty of care   2.27,
        7.8–7.9
    Trustee Act 1925, under the
        7.3–7.5
Investment
    advice, duty to obtain   3.32–3.42
    application of new powers   1.14,
        3.2–3.5
        precedent for exclusion of:
            App.III (Form C)
        precedent for inclusion of:
            App III (Form A)
    breach of trust   3.44–3.49
    checklist   3.43
    definition   1.34, 3.15–3.18
    diversify, duty to   3.30–3.31
    ethical grounds, on
        precedent   App III (Form B)
    express investment clauses   3.2
    general power of investment
        1.14–1.16, 3.11–3.14, 3.56–3.65

loans secured on land as   3.19–
    3.22
policy
    checklist   App III (Form M)
    reform, need for   3.1
'special statutory powers of
    investment', definition of
    1.16
Standard Investment Criteria
    3.23–3.31
    statutory duty of care   2.11–2.14,
        3.50–3.55
    precedent for claim alleging
        breach   App III (Form H)
    precedent for defence of claim
        alleging breach   App III
        (Form J)
suitability of investment   3.27–
    3.29
Trustee Investment Act 1961,
    under   3.7–3.10
unauthorised investment   3.44–
    3.49

Land
    acquisition *see* Acquisition of land
    definition   1.34
    loans secured on
        investment, as form of   3.19–
        3.22
Law Commission
    principle recommendations
        1.5–1.6
Loans
    secured on land
        investment, as form of   3.19–
        3.22

Nominees
    appointment   1.19–1.20, 5.35,
        5.37
        statutory duty of care   2.19–
        2.23, 2.55–2.59
    remuneration   5.20–5.24, 5.39,
        6.38–6.42
    statutory duty of care, application of,
        to   2.35

Parliamentary progress of Act
1.7–1.9, App II
Protectors
rights in the trust   2.38

Reform, general need for   1.2–1.4
see also Law Commission: principle
recommendations
Remuneration   1.21
administration expense, as an
6.30–6.31
agents, of   5.20–5.24, 6.38–6.42
agreement in writing
precedent   App III (Form G)
application of new powers
where express charging clause
exists   6.13
where no provision exists   6.20
charitable trustees, of   6.32–6.34
custodians, of   5.20–5.24, 5.39,
6.38–6.42
expenses, reimbursement of
6.35–6.37   .
gift, as a   6.17–6.19
lay trustees, for services capable of
being performed by   6.14–
6.16
nominees, of   5.20–5.24, 5.39,
6.38–6.42
professional capacity, of trustees
acting in a   6.23–6.24
definition of 'professional
capacity'   6.27–6.29
prohibition by previous law
exceptions   6.5–6.7
'reasonable remuneration',
definition of   6.25–6.26
reform, need for   6.1–6.3
reimbursement of expenses
6.35–6.37
standard professional charging
clause
default, as   6.4
precedent: App III (Form F)
trust corporations, of   6.21–6.22
Repeals and amendments   1.28–
1.31

Resulting trustees
general power of investment,
application of, to   3.65
statutory duty of care, application of,
to   2.36
Reversionary interests
statutory duty of care   2.28–2.29
Review, duty to
delegation arrangements   2.22,
5.40–5.43
existing trusts   2.70–2.72
Royal Assent, date of   1.9

Scope of the Act   1.10–1.13
Standard Investment Criteria   3.23–
3.31
Statutory duty of care
aim   2.1–2.2
application   1.13, 1.23–1.24, 1.33,
2.10
acquisition of land, to   2.15–
2.18, 4.22–4.24
audit, to   2.28–2.29
bare trustees, to   2.35
compounding of liabilities, to
2.24–2.26
constructive trustees, to   2.36
delegation, to   2.19–2.23, 2.55–
2.59, 5.40–5.43
breach of duty, effect of   5.46
precedent for claim alleging
breach   App III
(Form I)
existing trusts, to   2.70–2.72
insurance, to   2.27, 7.8–7.9
investment, to   2.11–2.14, 3.50–
3.55
precedent for claim alleging
breach: App III
(Form H)
precedent for defence of claim
alleging breach   App III
(Form J)
nominees, to   2.35
omissions, to   2.30–2.32
protectors, to   2.38
resulting trustees, to   2.36

Statutory duty of care – *cont*
  application – *cont*
    reversionary interests, to   2.28–
      2.29
    review, to
      delegation arrangements, of
        2.22, 5.40–5.43
      existing trusts, of   2.70–2.72
      strict settlements, to   2.37
      'trustees', to   2.34
      valuation, to   2.28–2.29
    breach of duty, remedies for
      2.60–2.68
    exclusion of duty   1.8, 2.39–2.47
      precedent   App III (Form K)
    limitation of duty
      precedent   App III (Form L)

    standard of care   1.25, 2.3–2.9
      common law duty and statutory
        duty compared   2.48–2.54
Strict settlements
  statutory duty of care, application of,
    to   2.37

Tenants for life
  statutory duty of care, application of,
    to   2.37
'Trustee'
  definition   1.34, 2.34

Valuation
  statutory duty of care   2.28–2.29